iStreetPhoto

iStreetPhoto

Copyright © 2016 by Bob Bovin

Bovin Design HB, Lilla Nygatan 15, Stockholm

All rights reserved. No part of this book may be reproduced

Homepage: www.bovin.nu/bob

Email: bobt@bovin.nu

Print and distribution: CreateSpace an Amazon company

ISBN: 978-91-981019-1-1

iStreetPhoto

Bob Bovin

Bob Bovin was at a young age a press photographer in Sweden, and got early on a documentary view on life. The situations of modern ways of living are his favorite themes. Bob has been walking the streets of some cities of Sweden the last five years and he shows here some of his pictures.

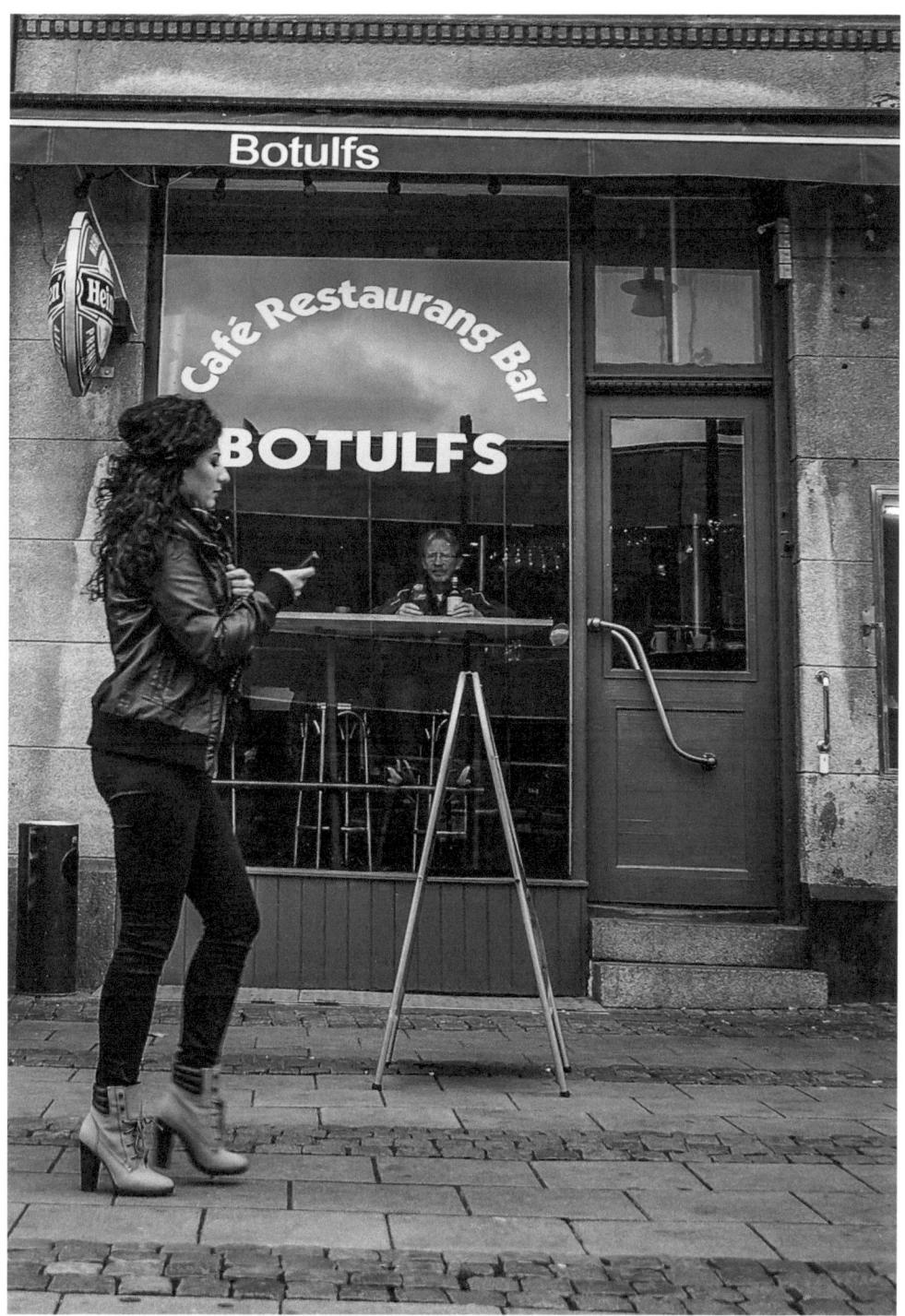

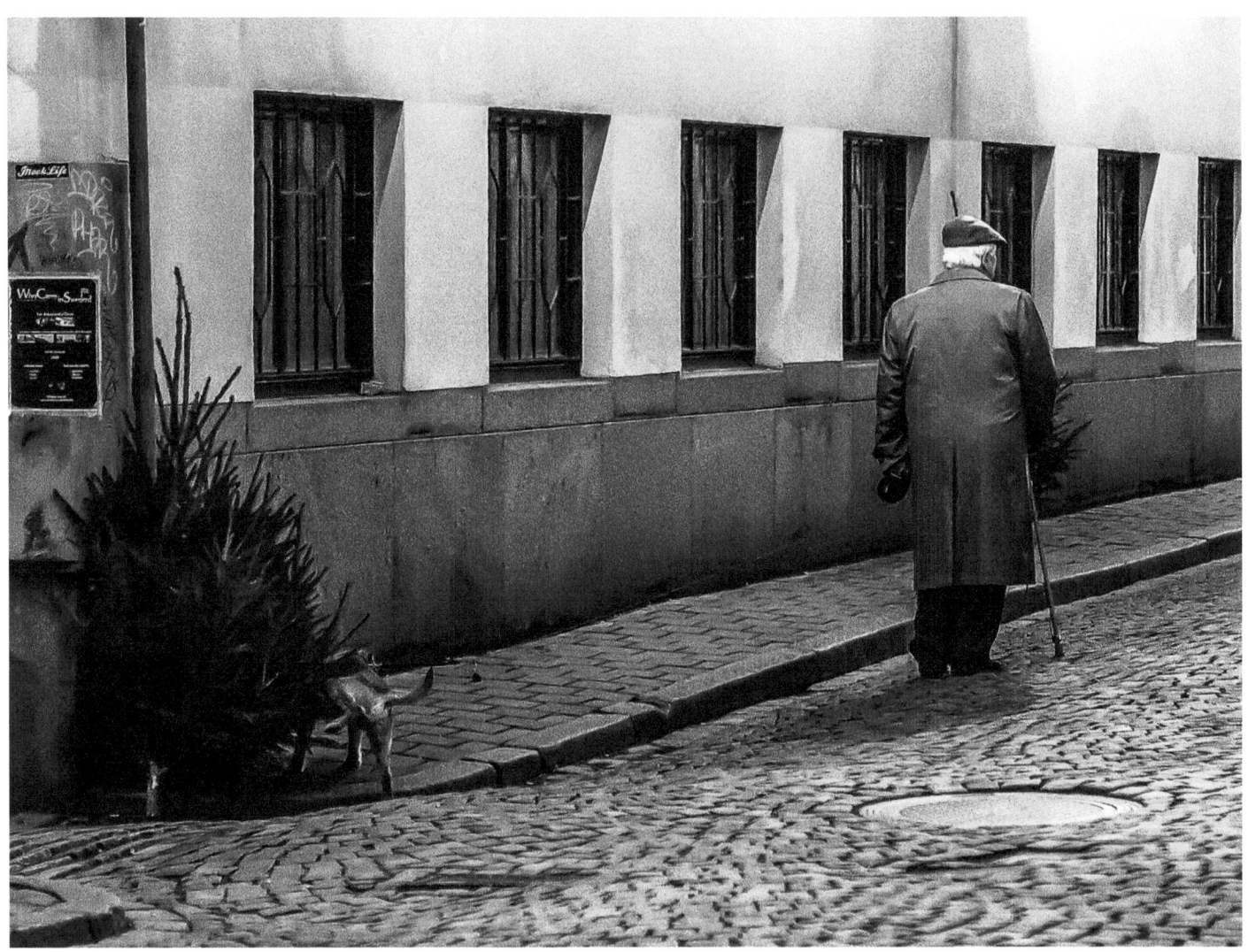

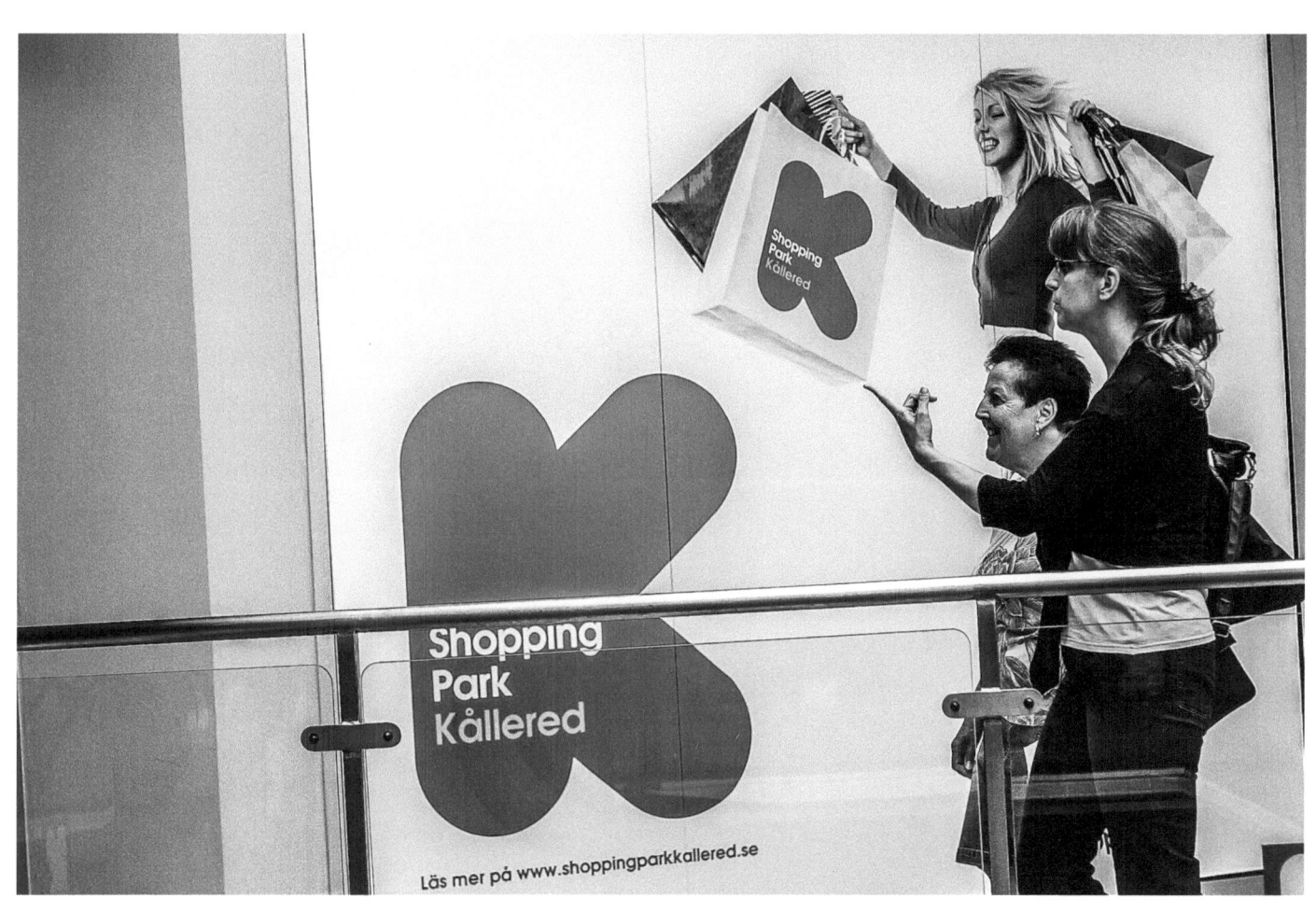

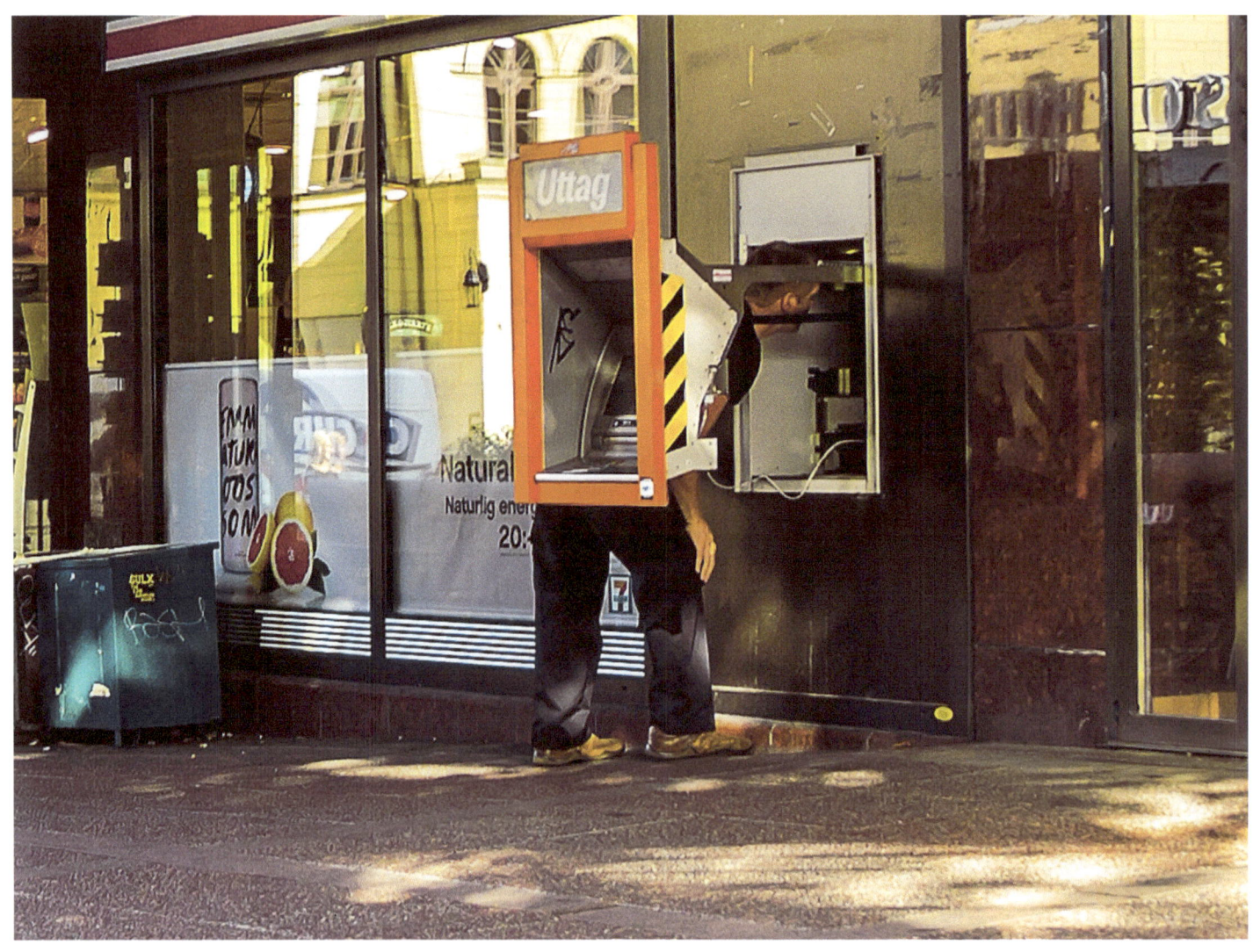

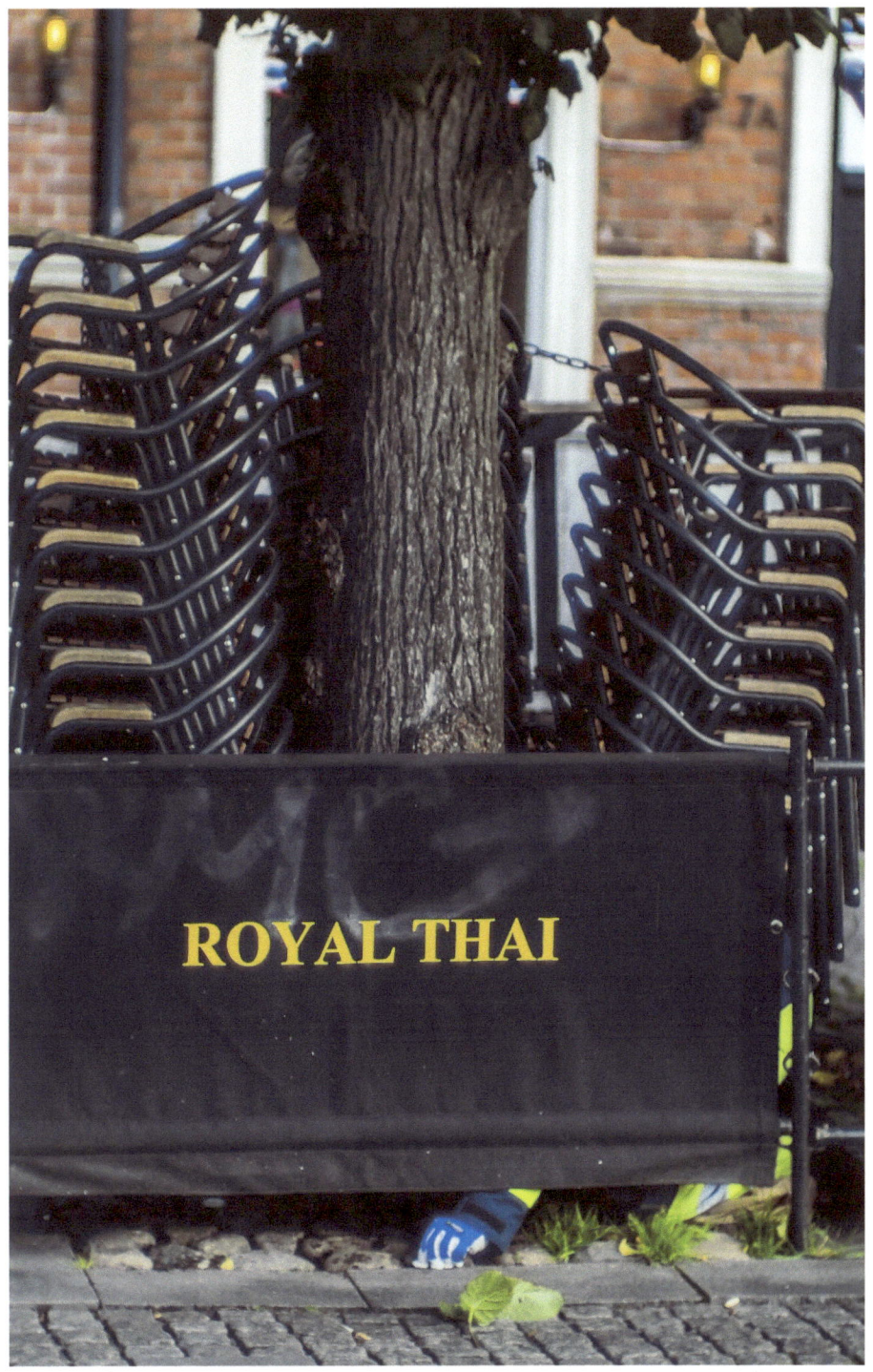

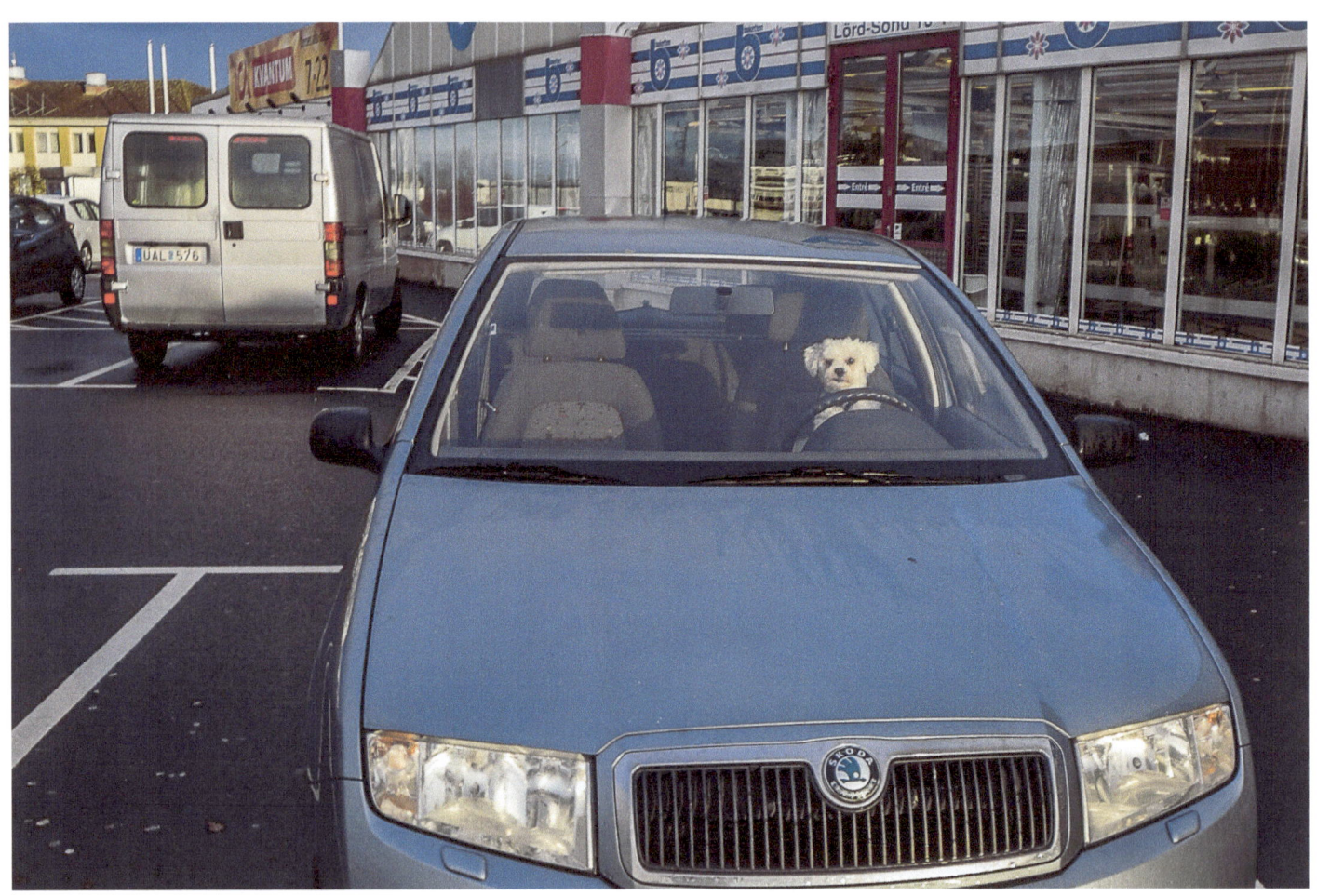

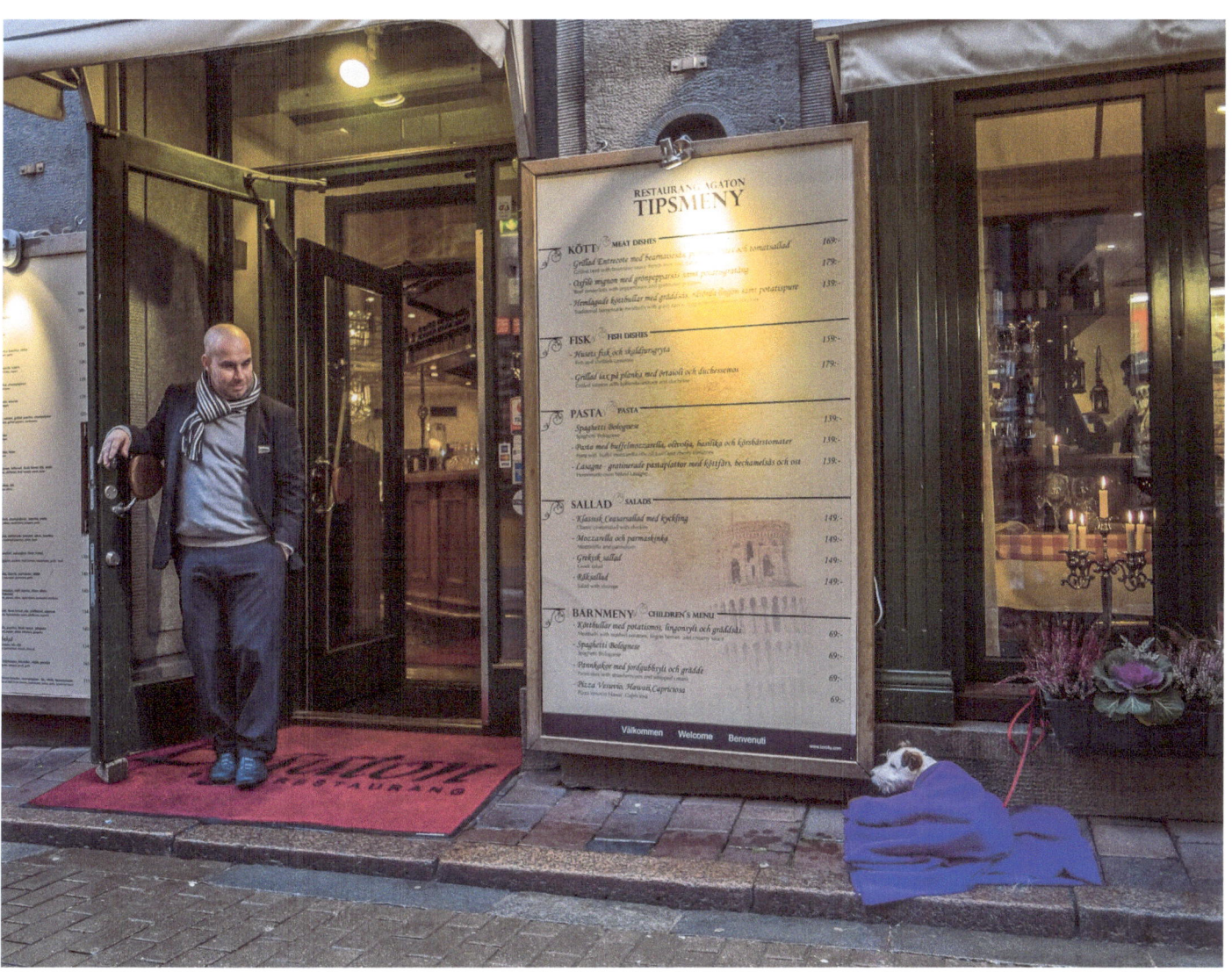

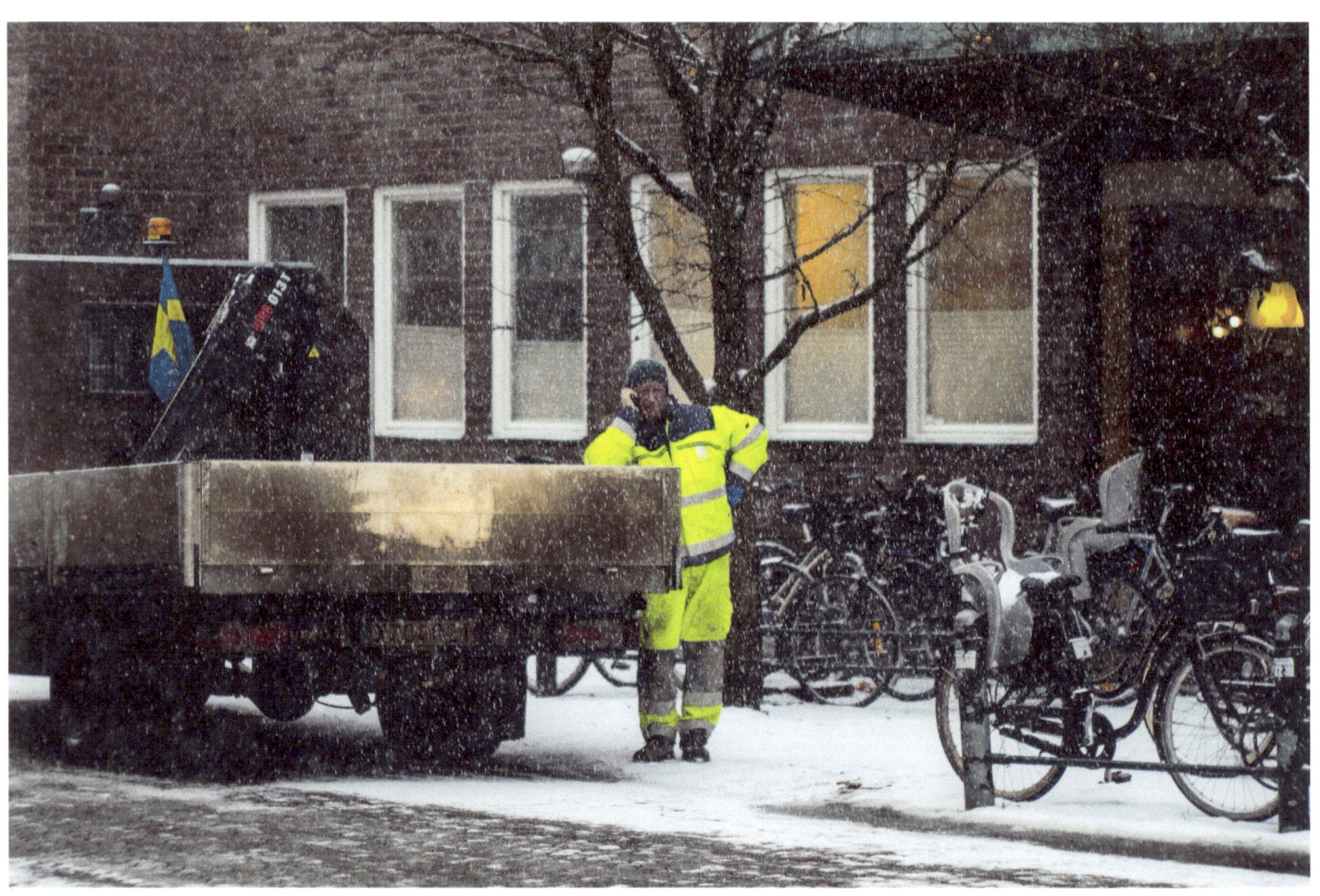

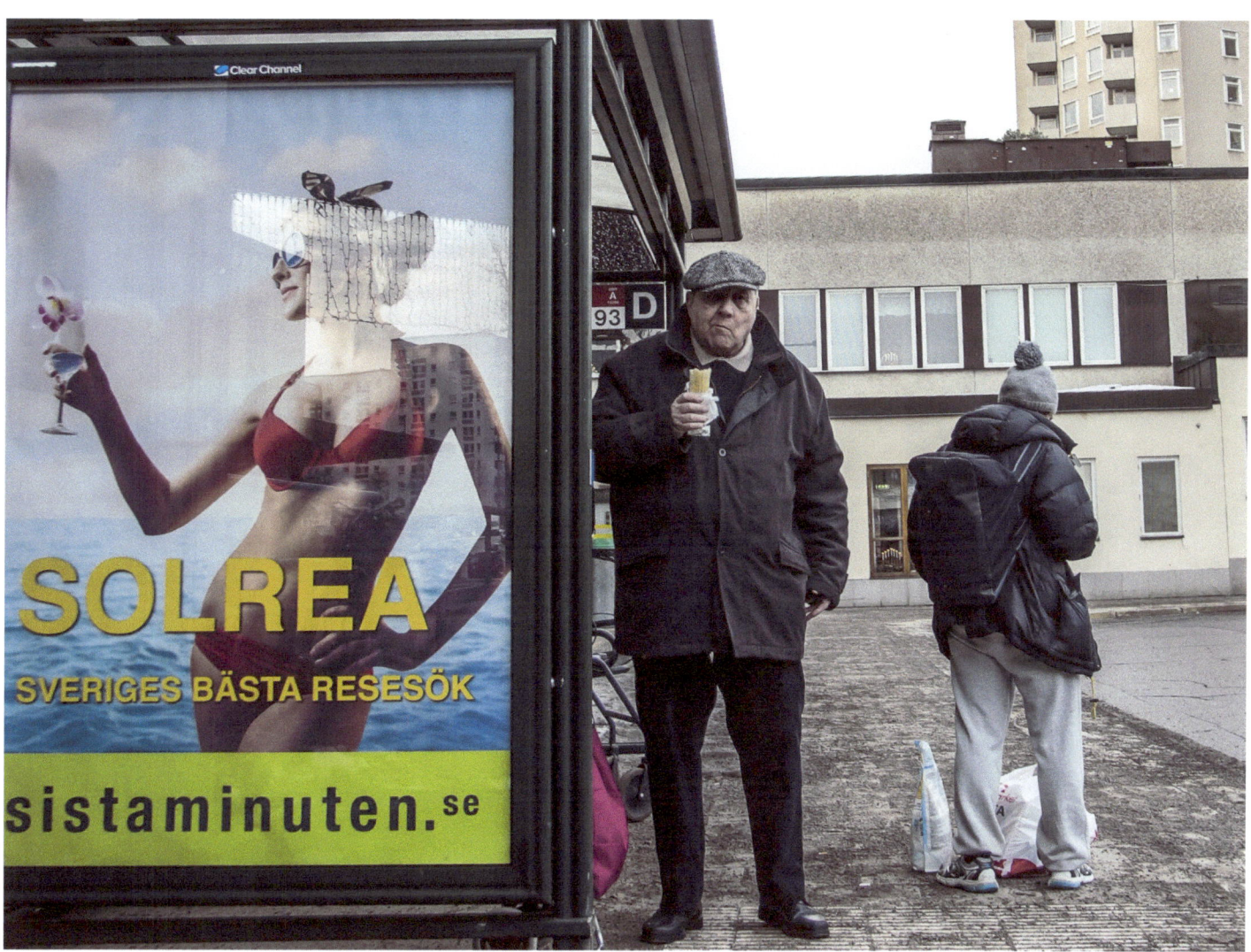

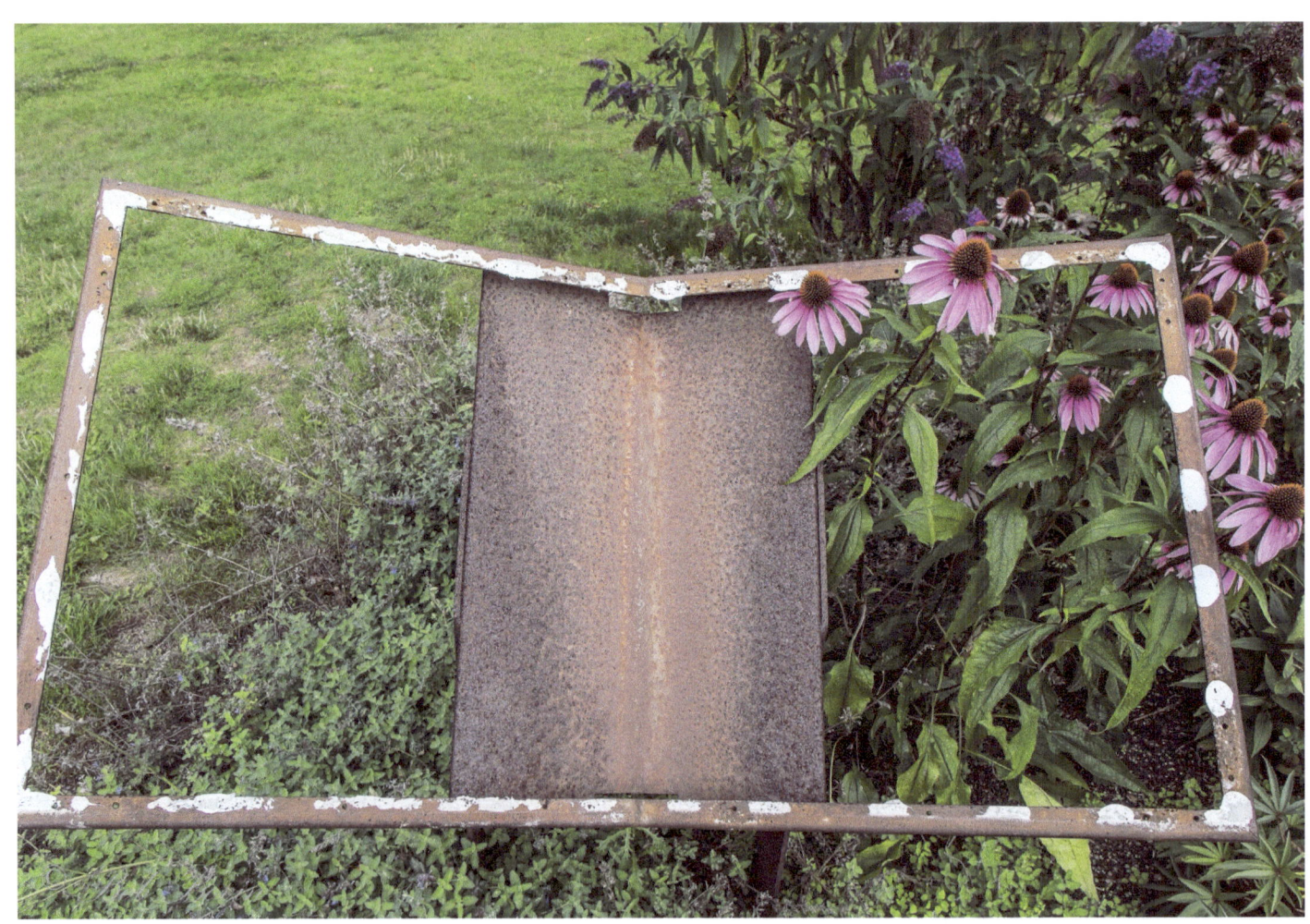

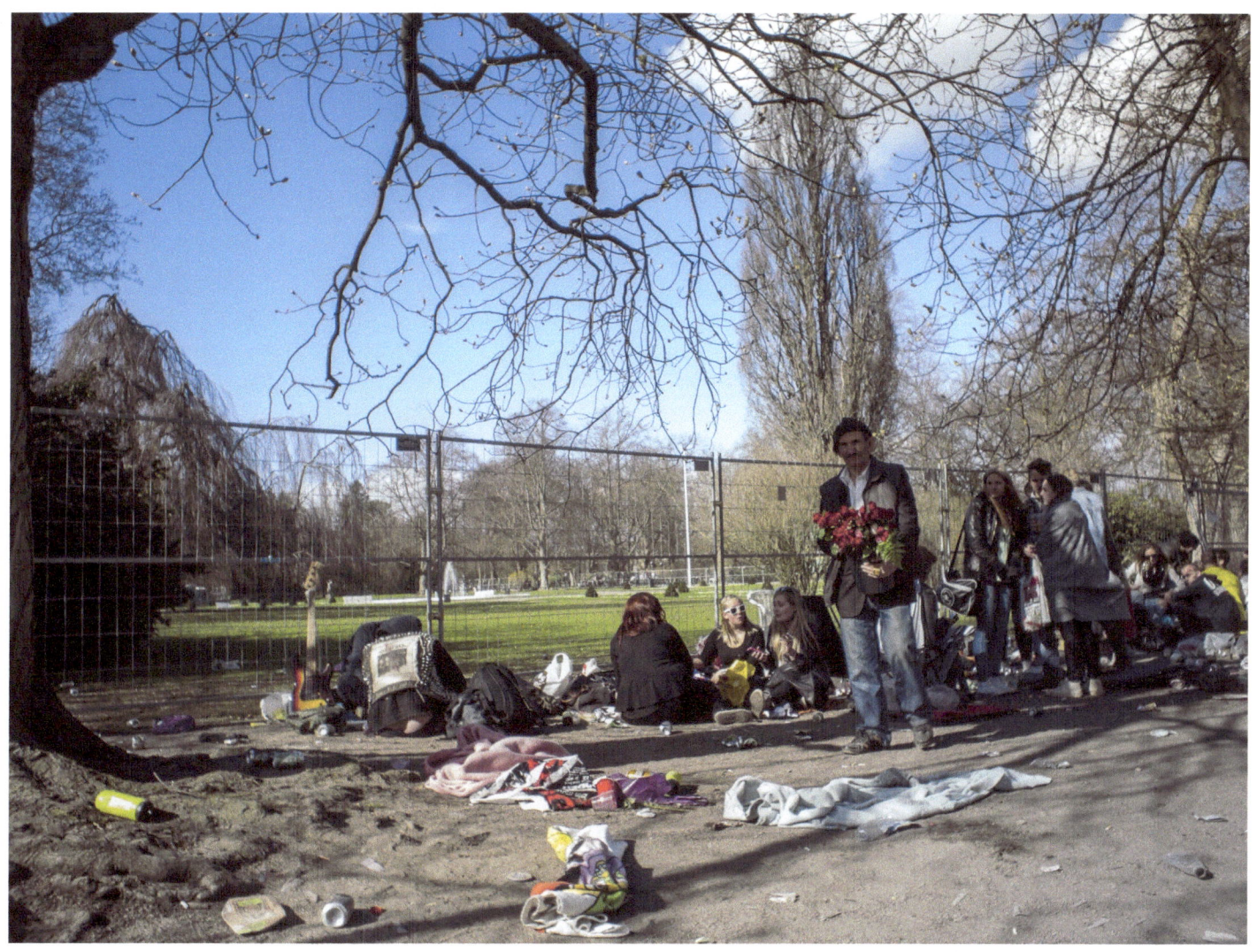

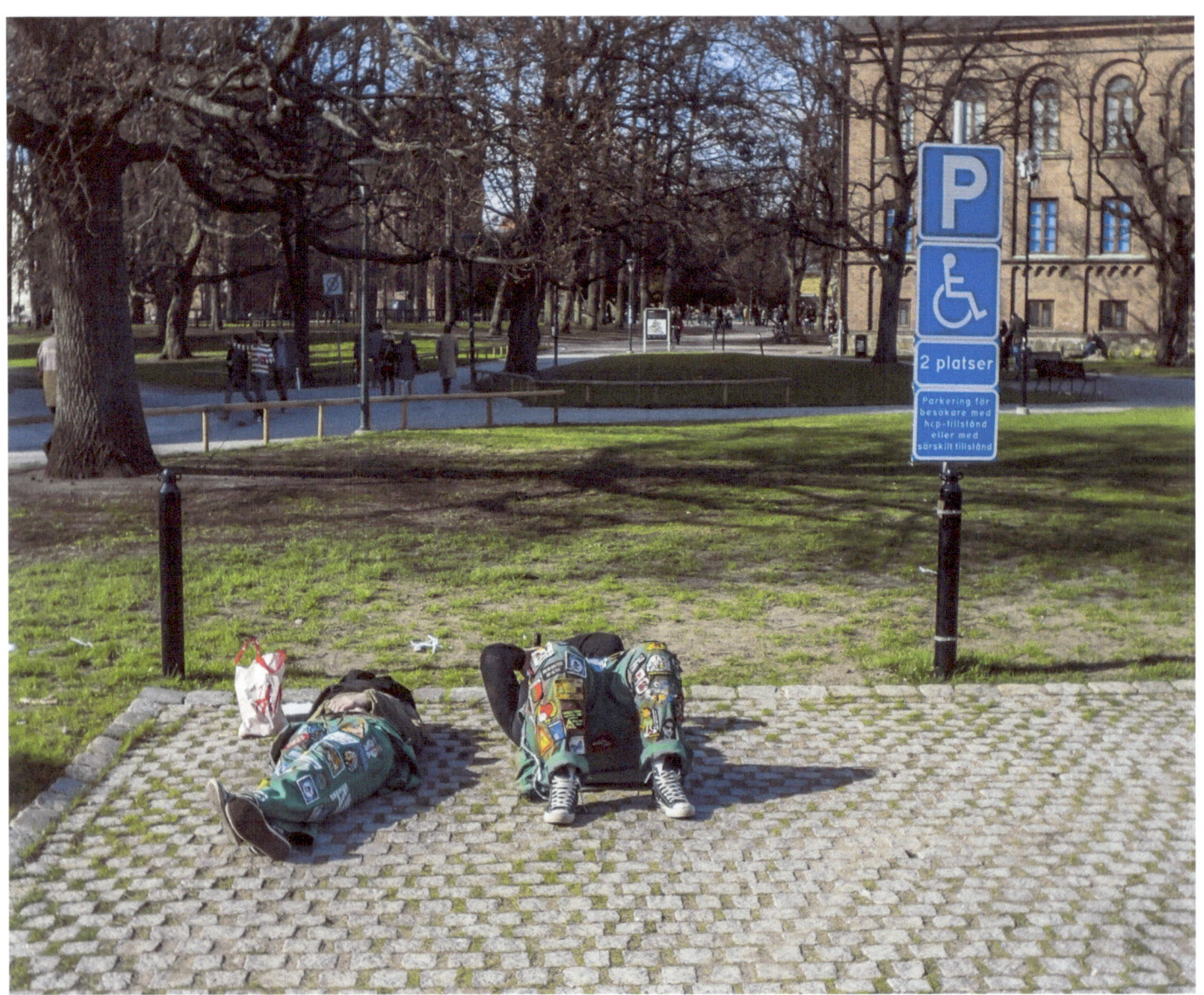

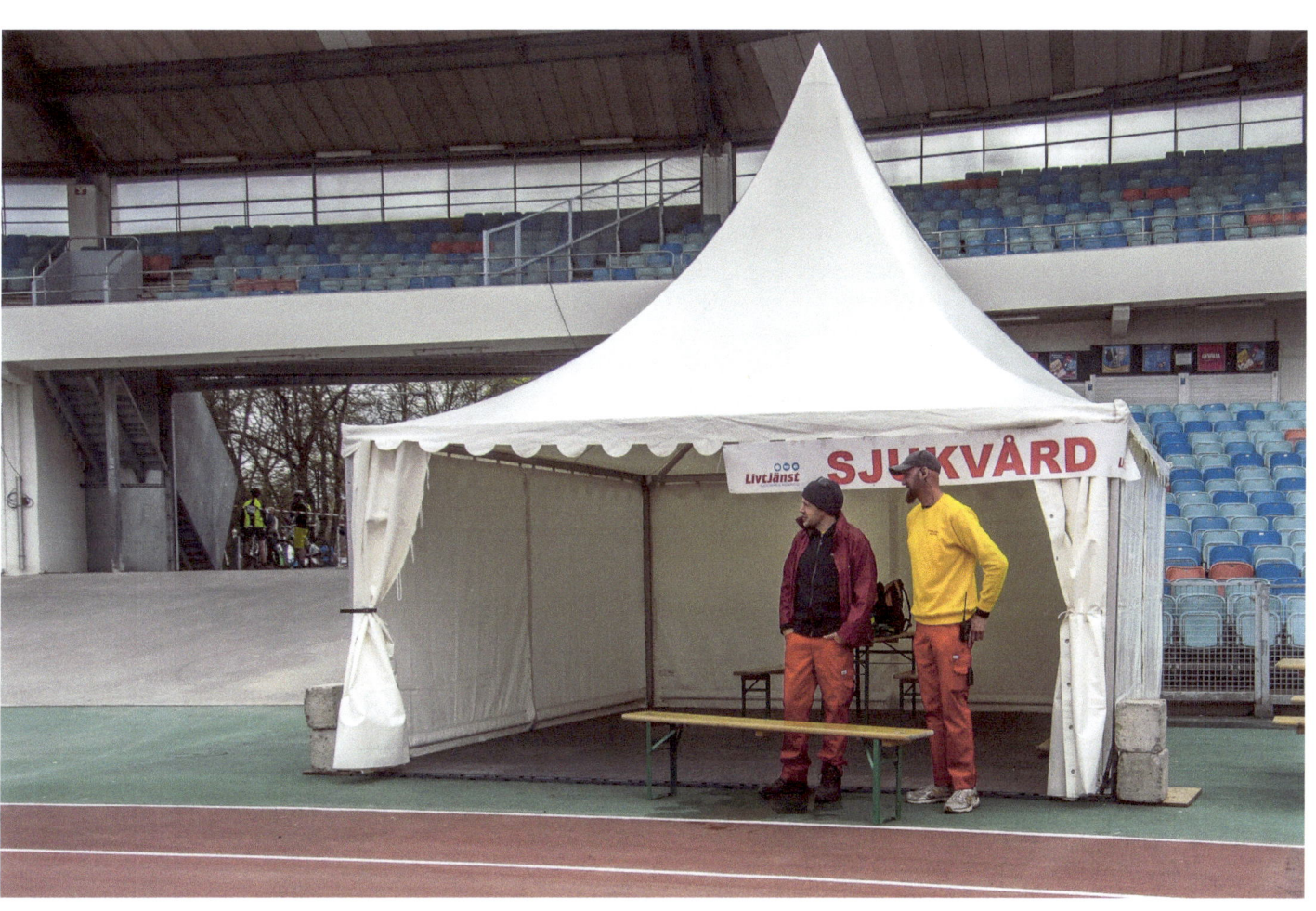

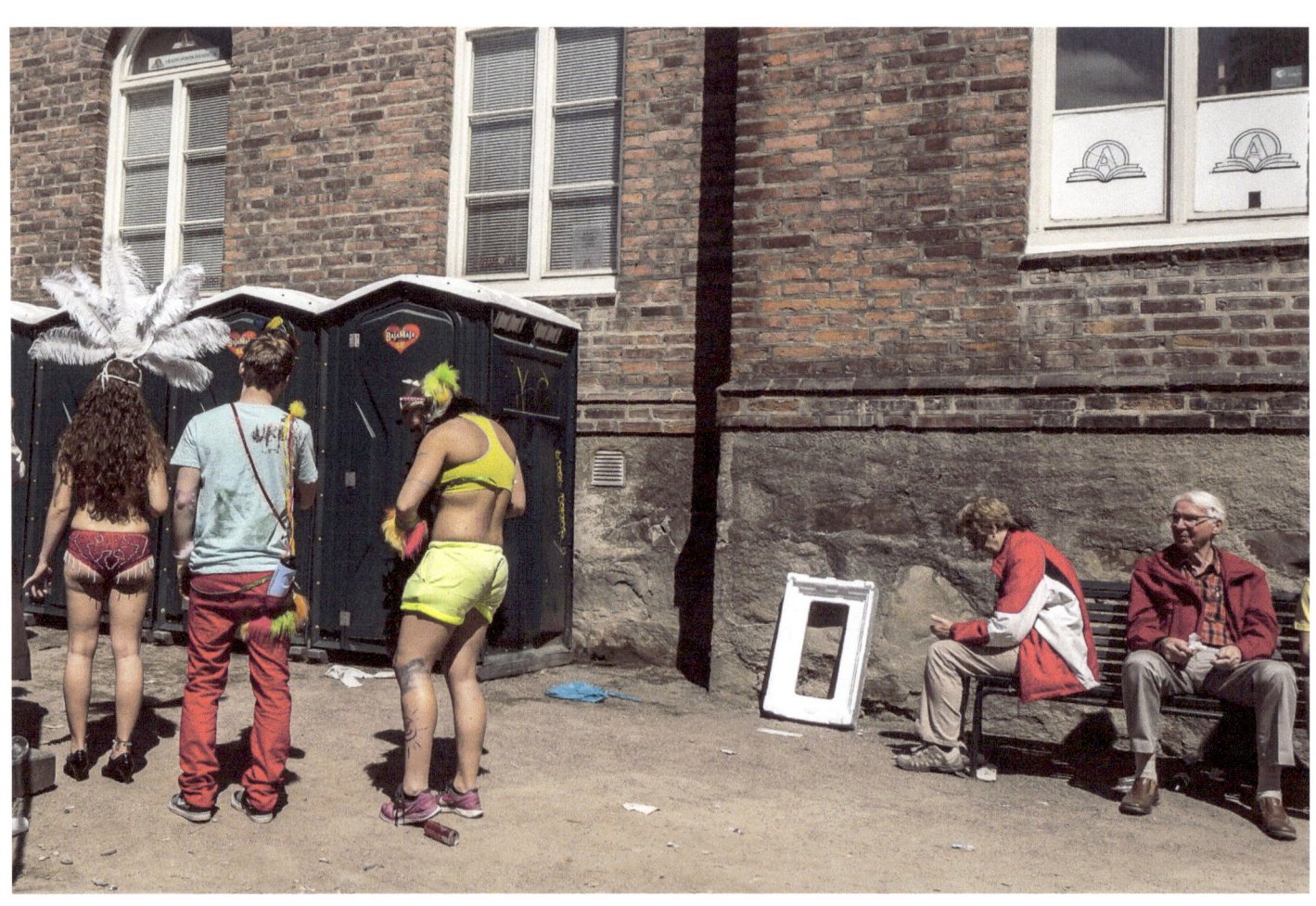

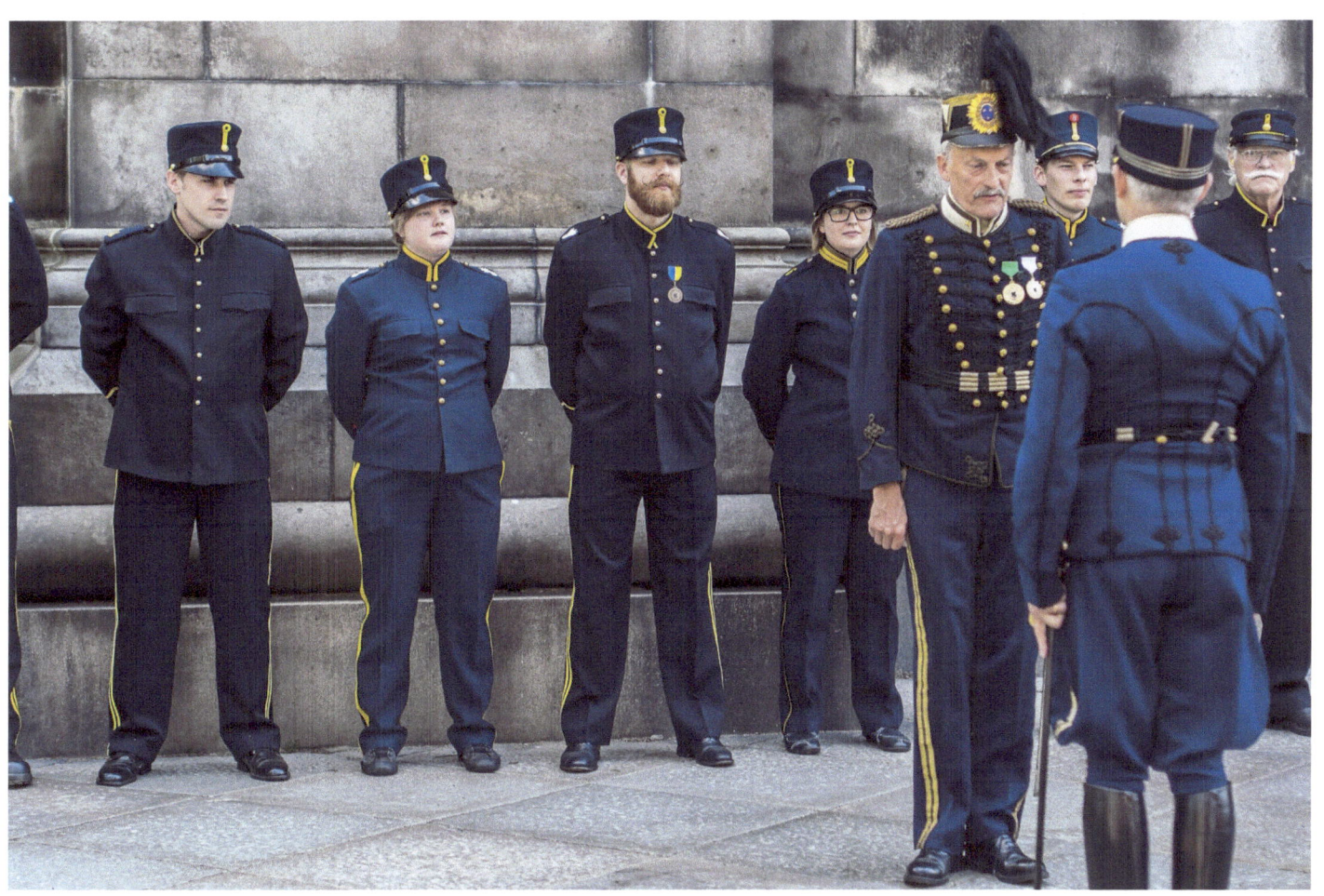

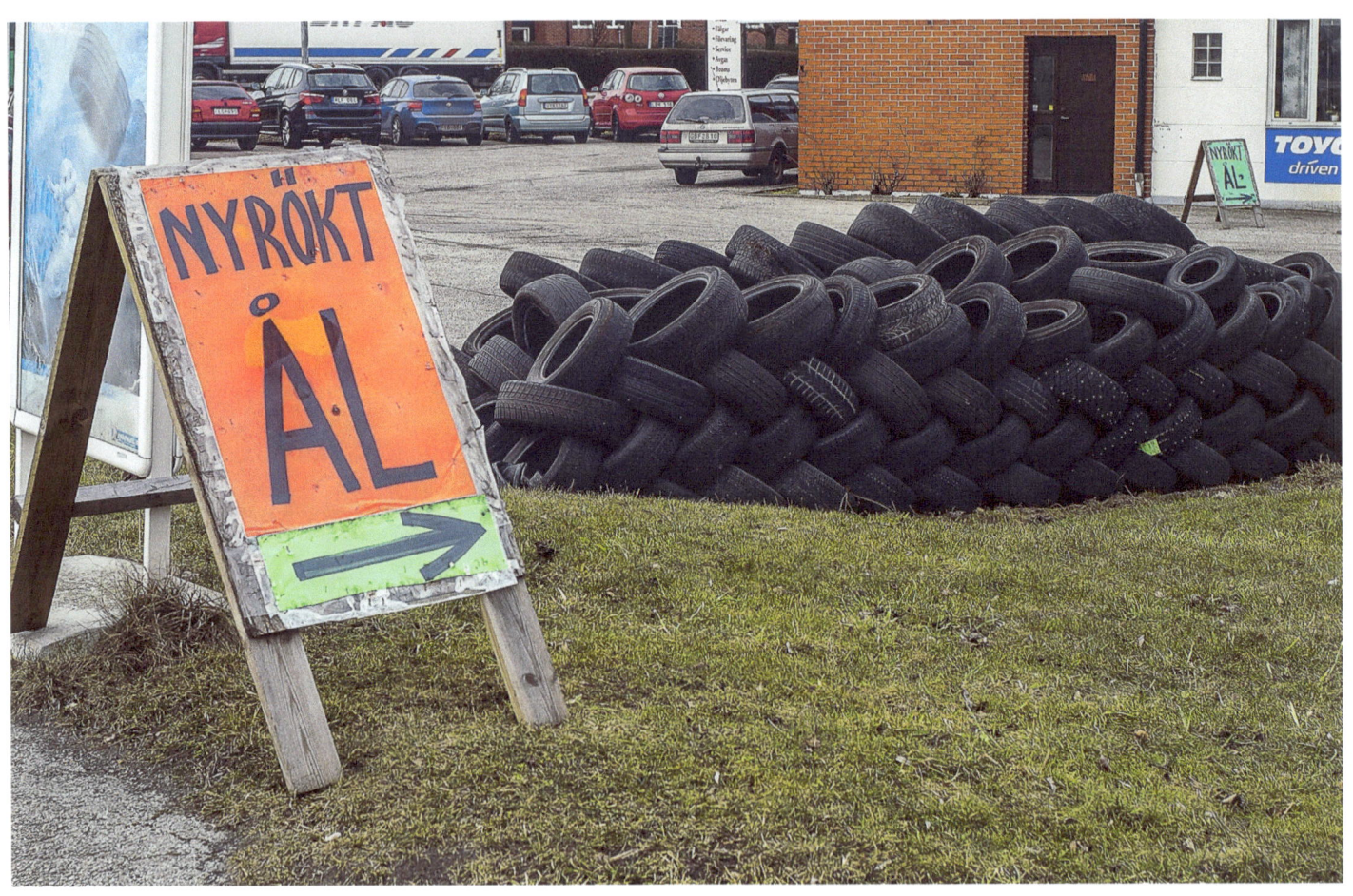

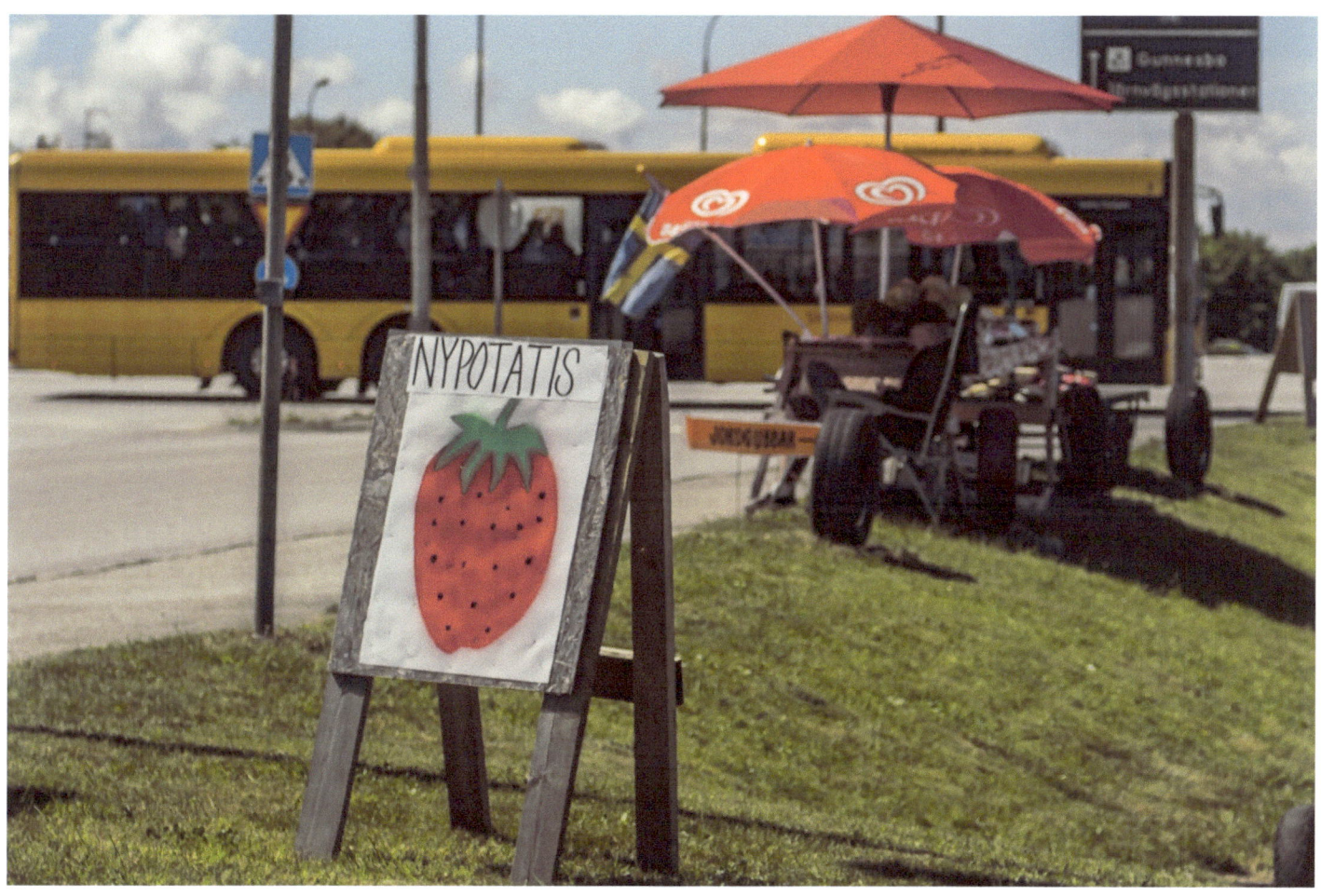

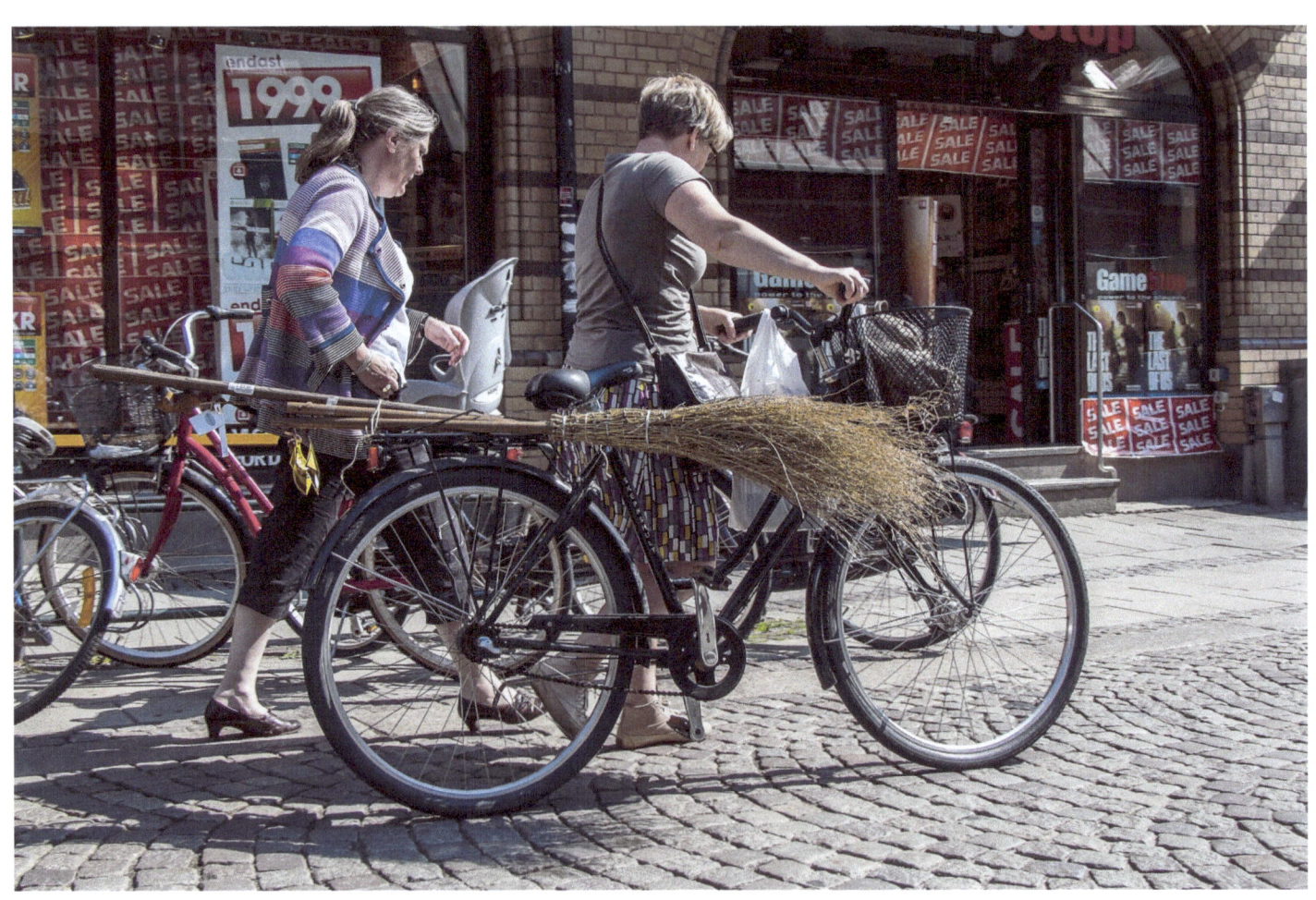

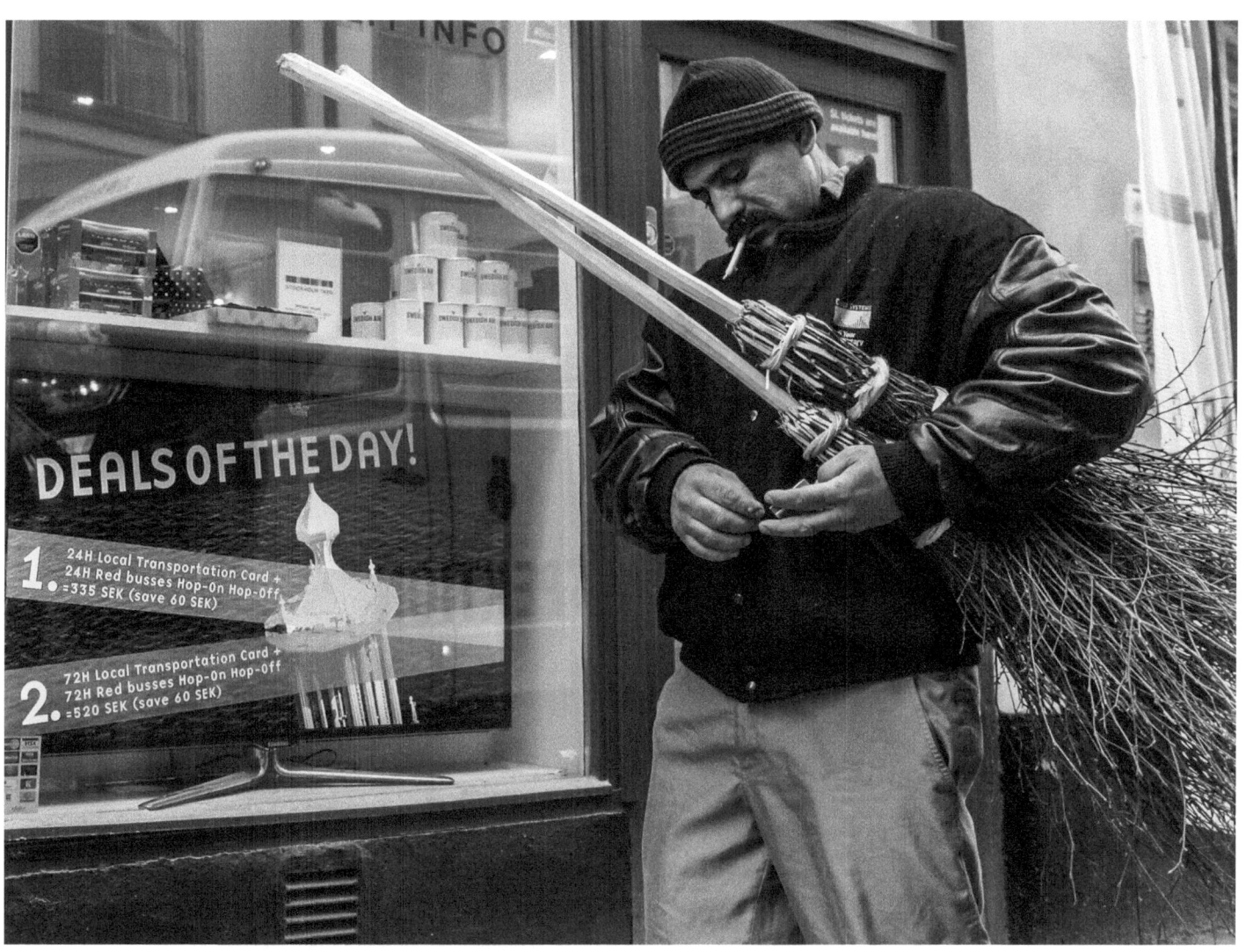

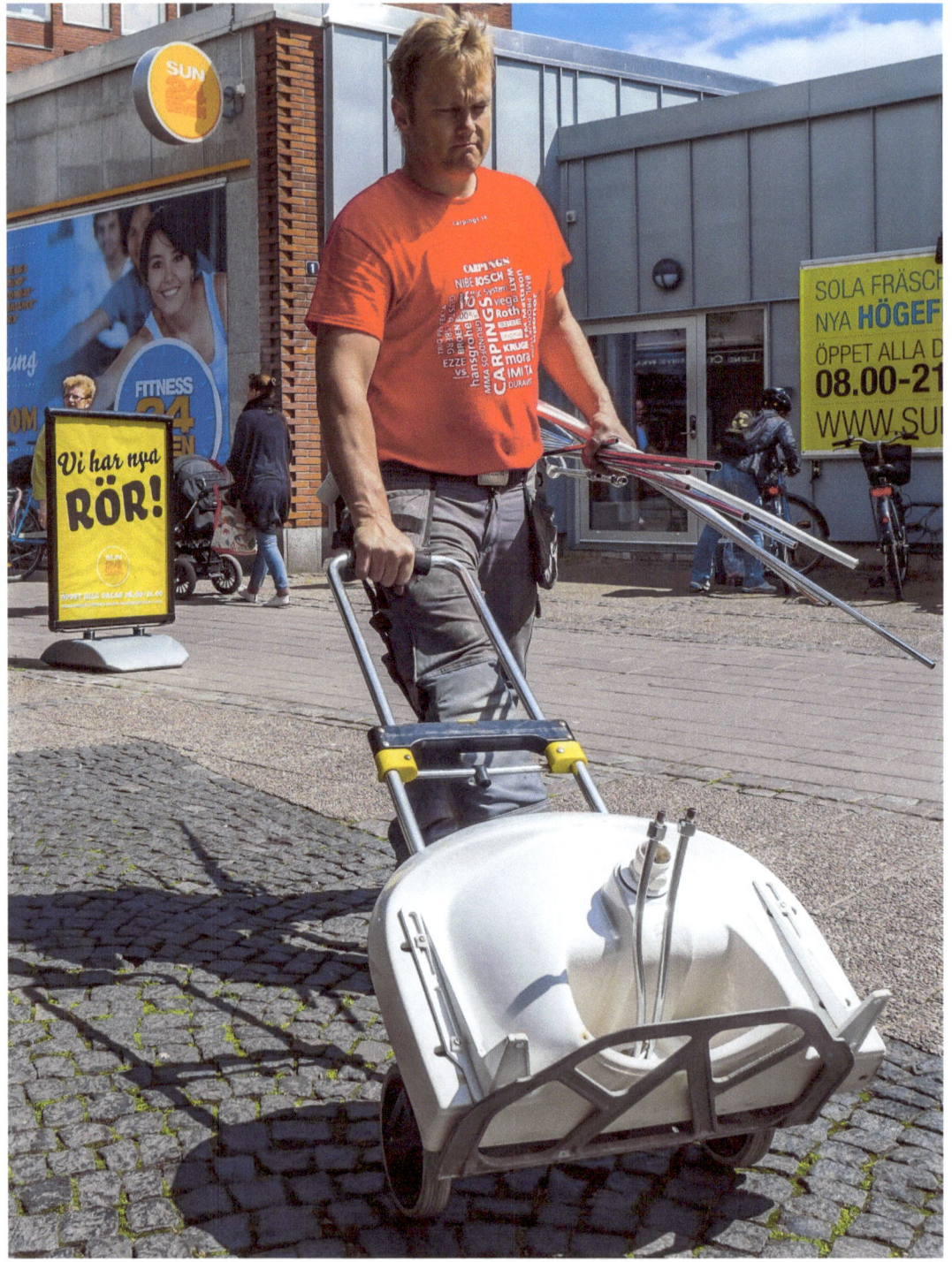

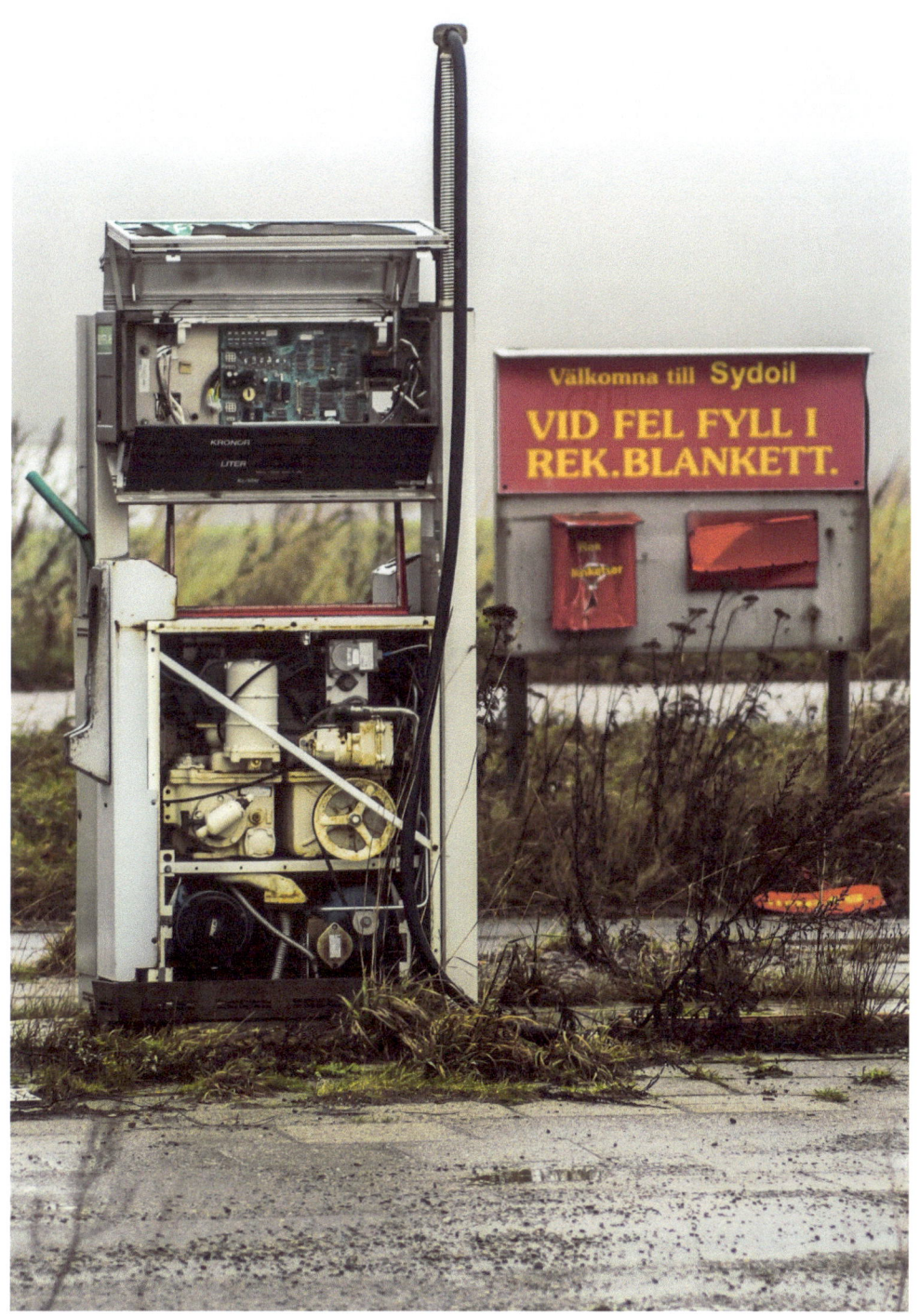

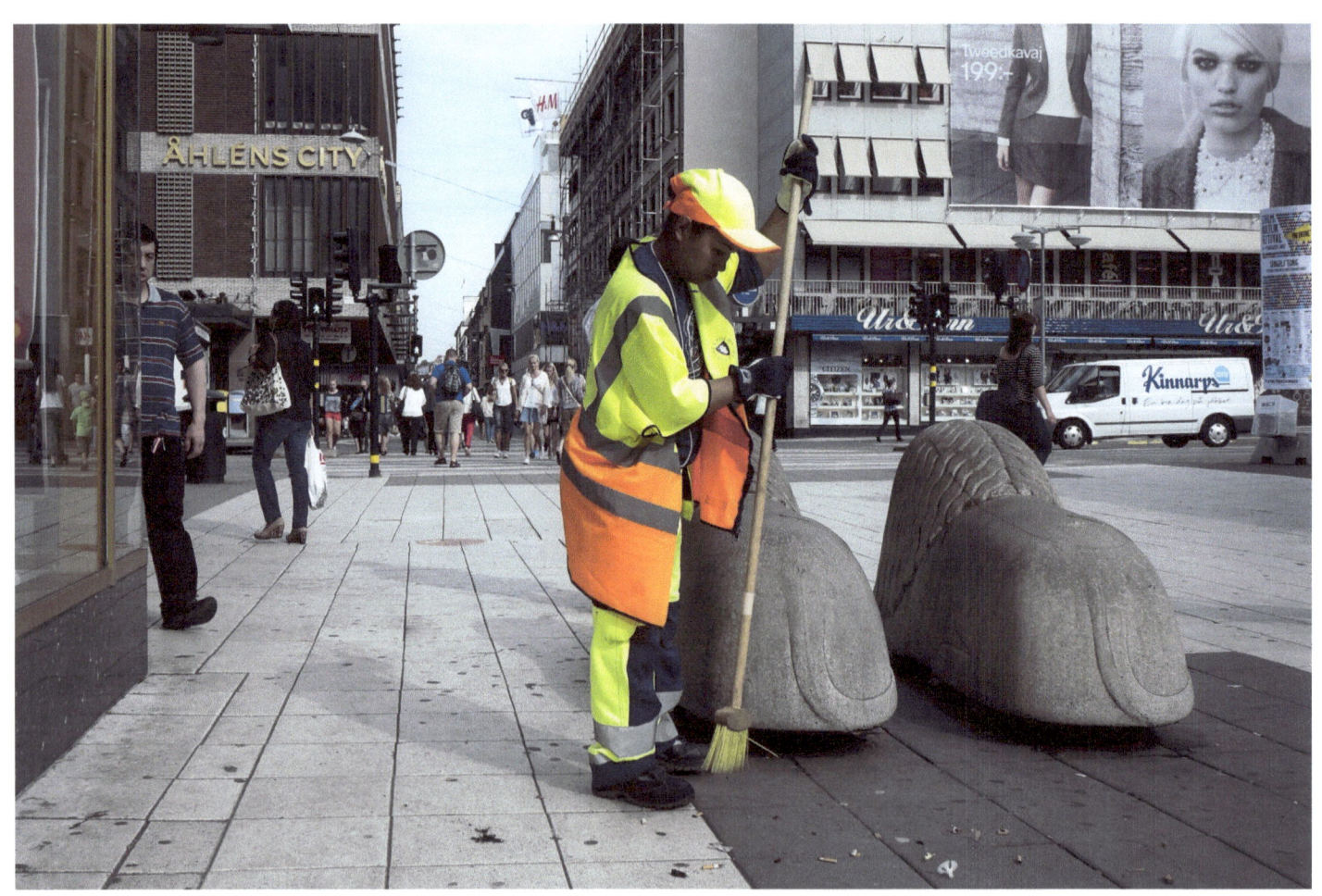

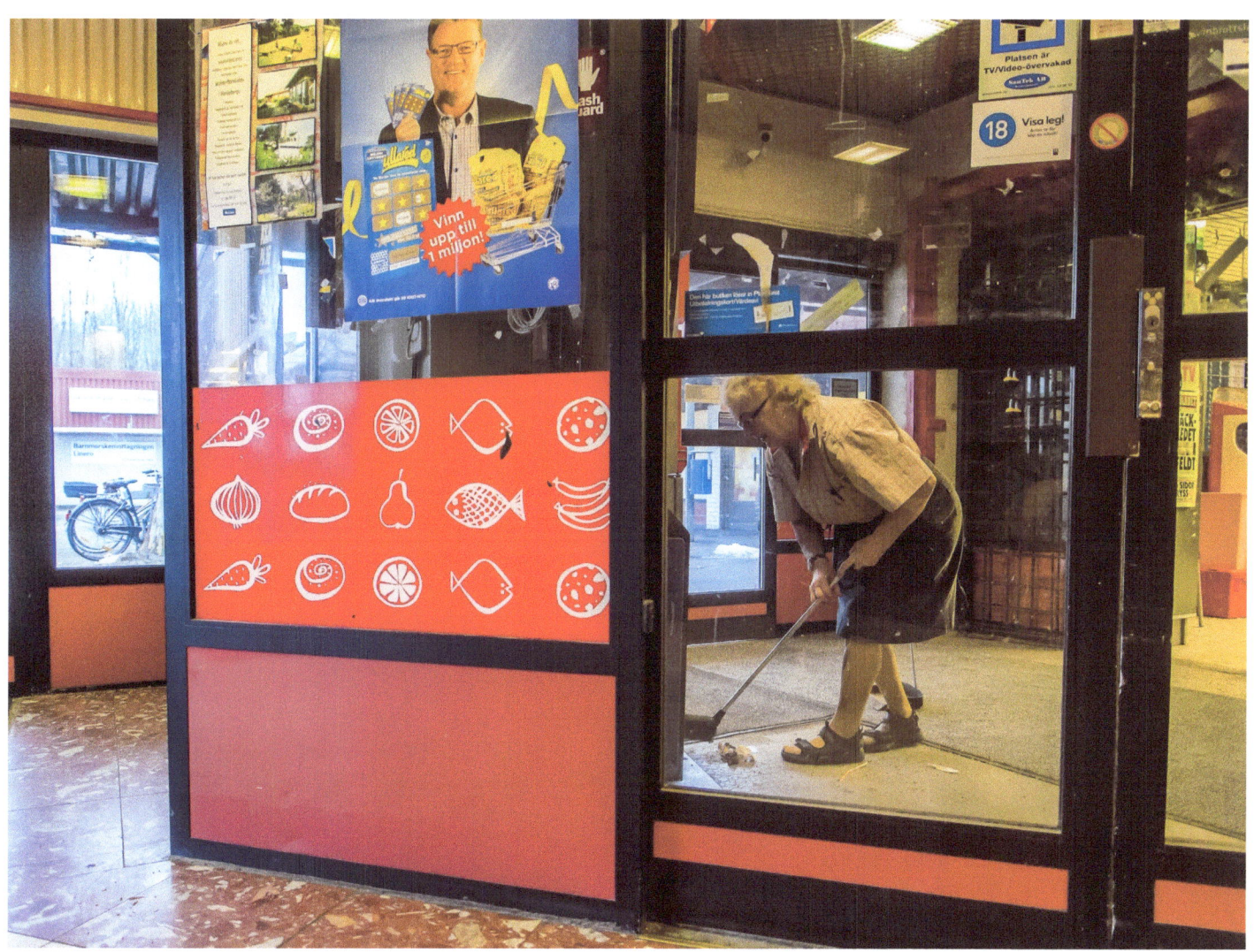

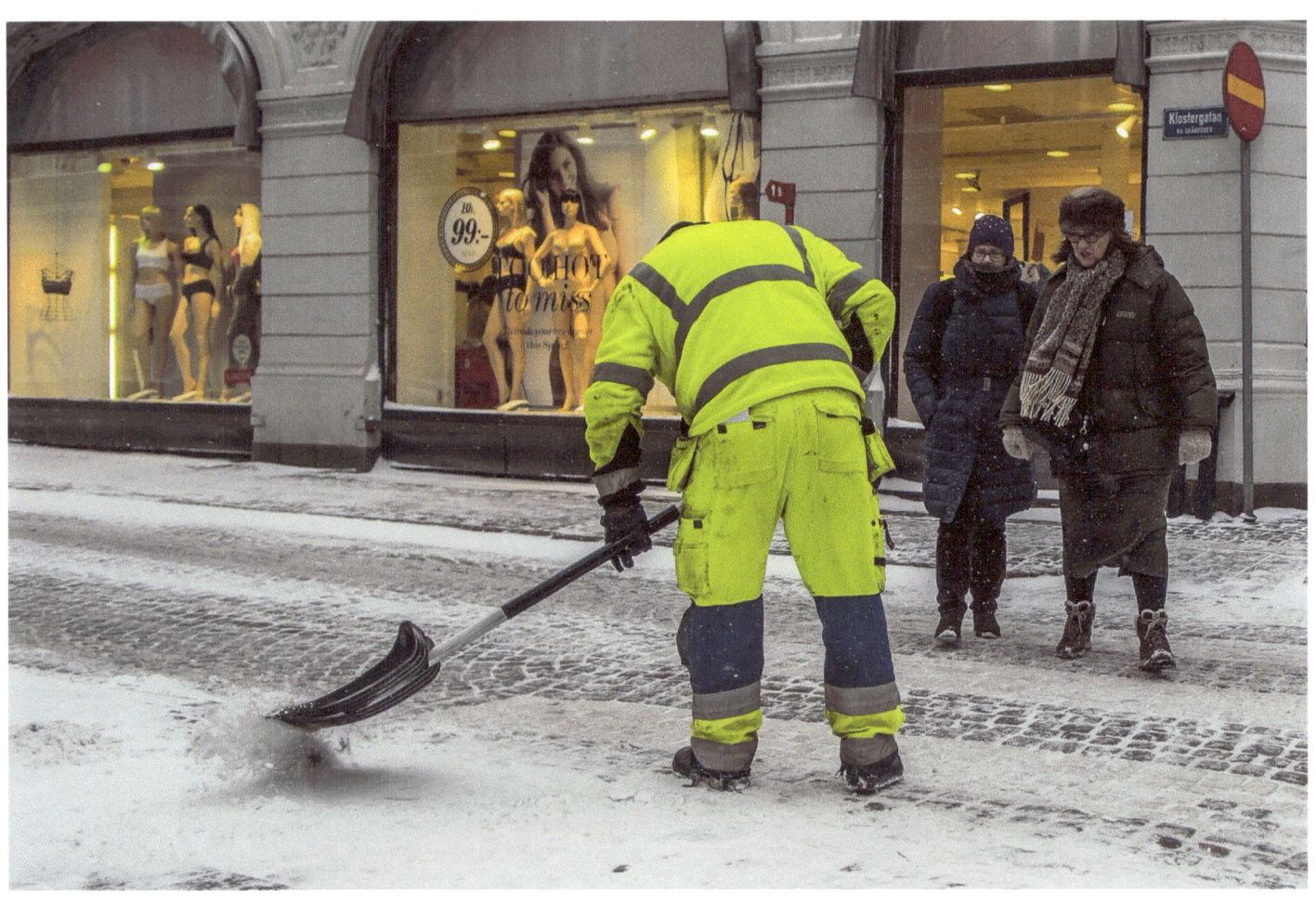

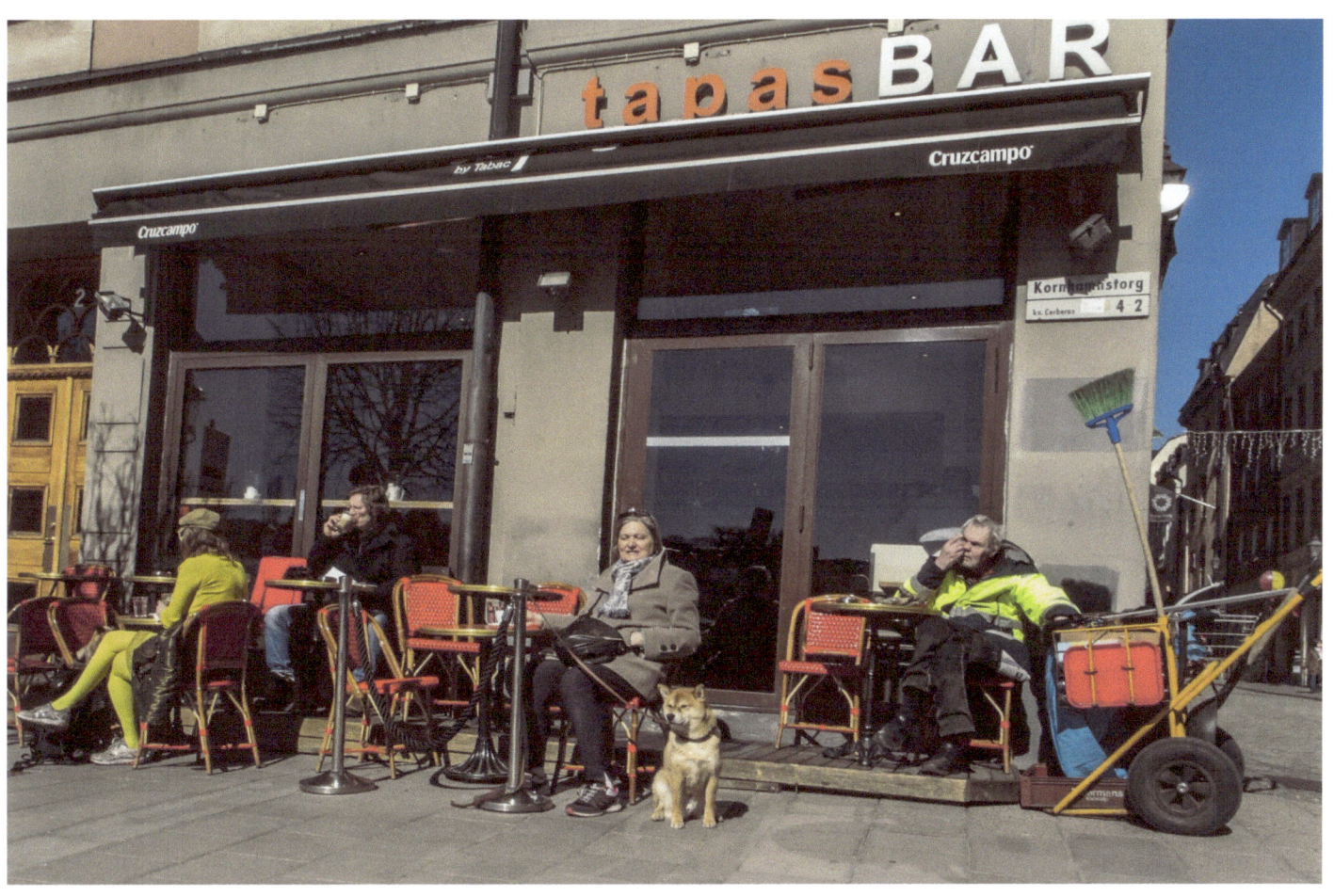

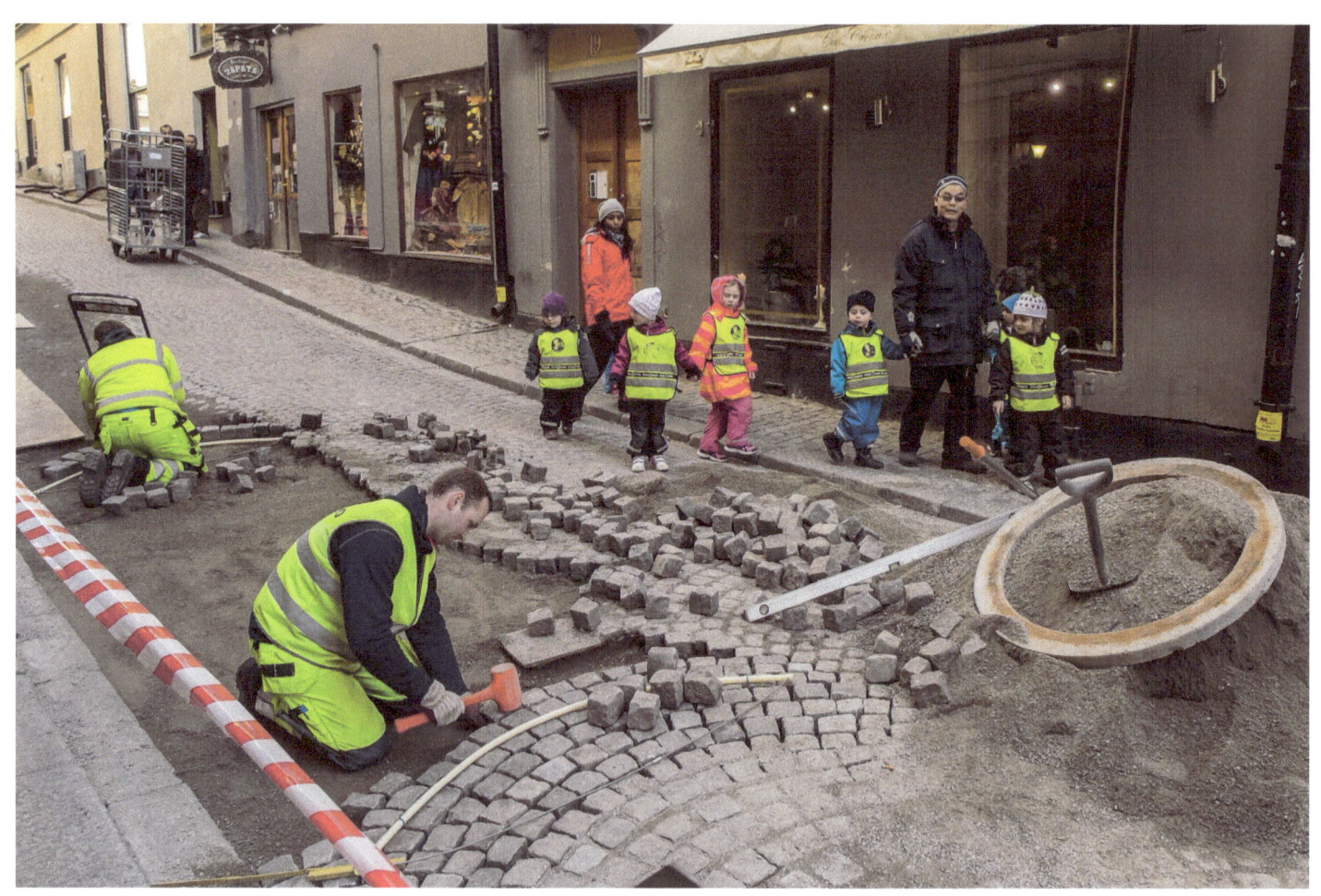

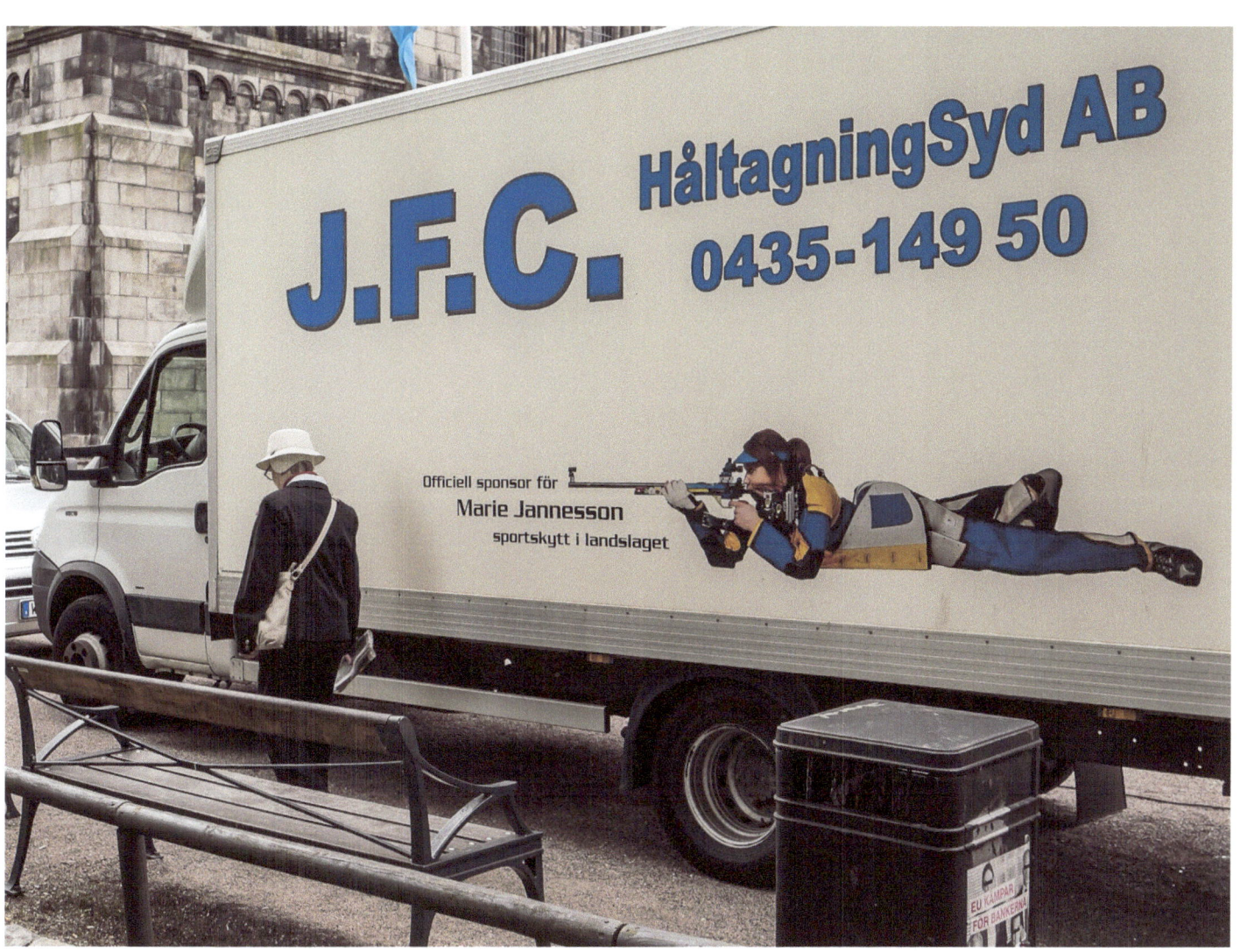

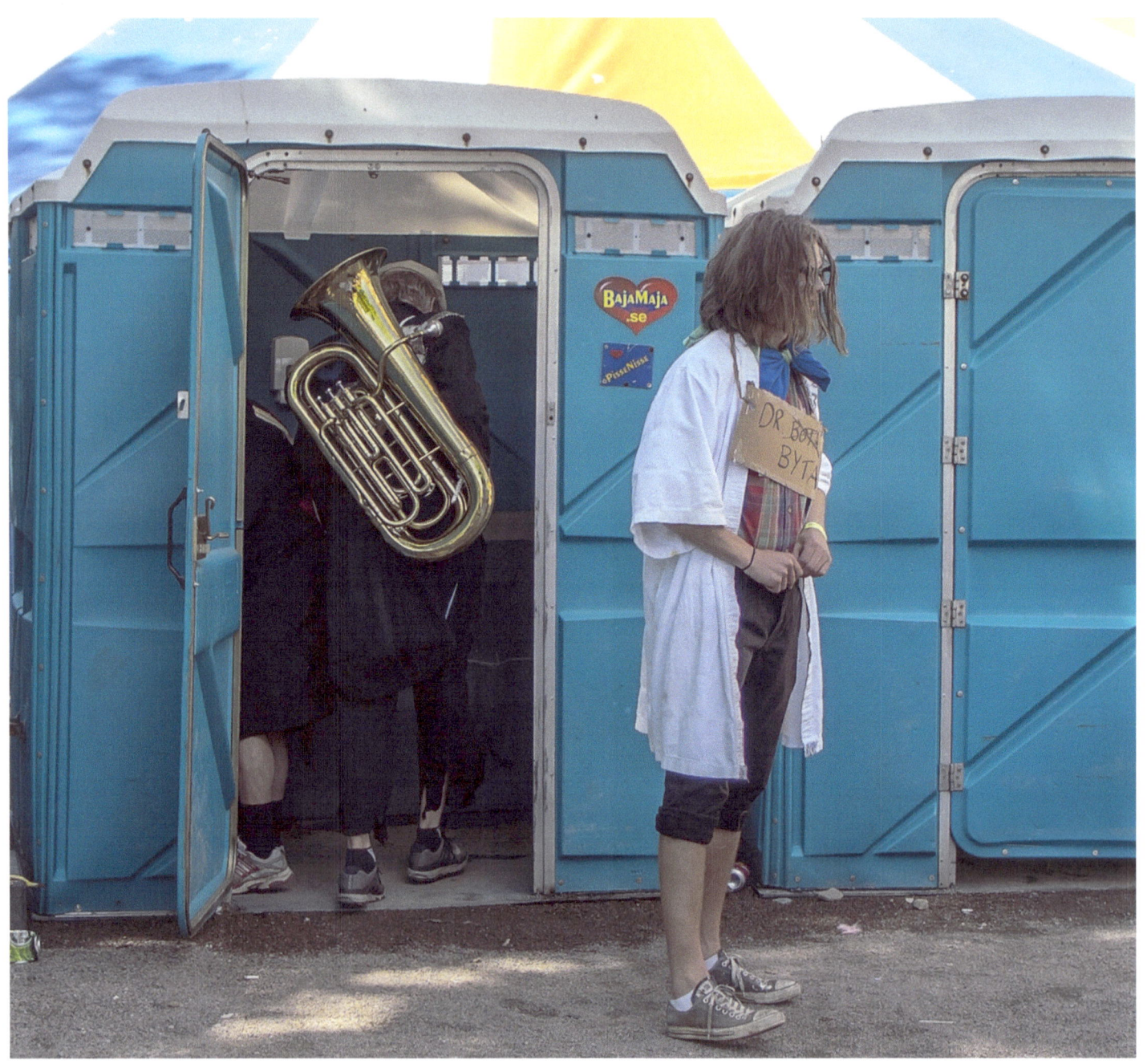

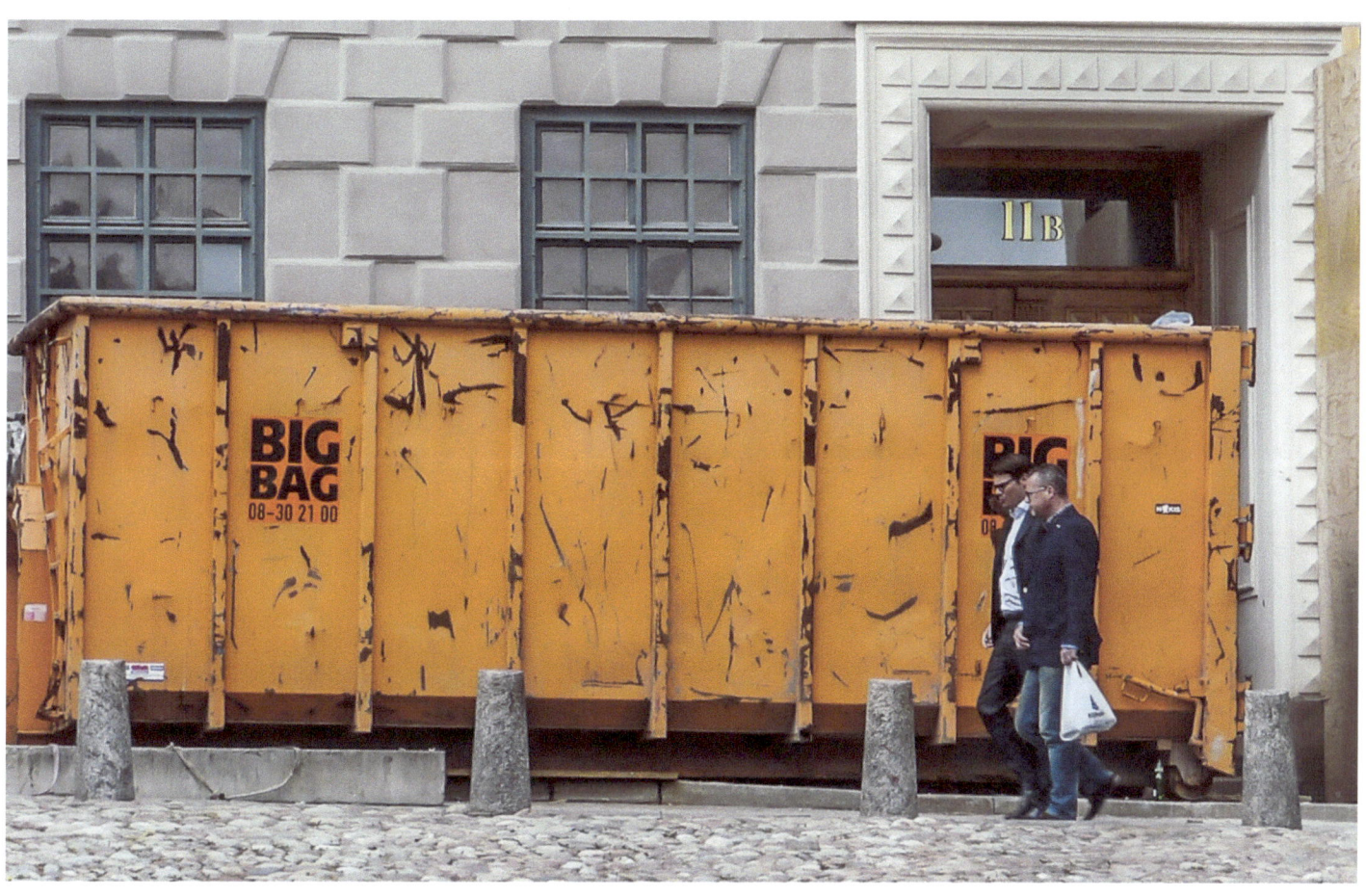

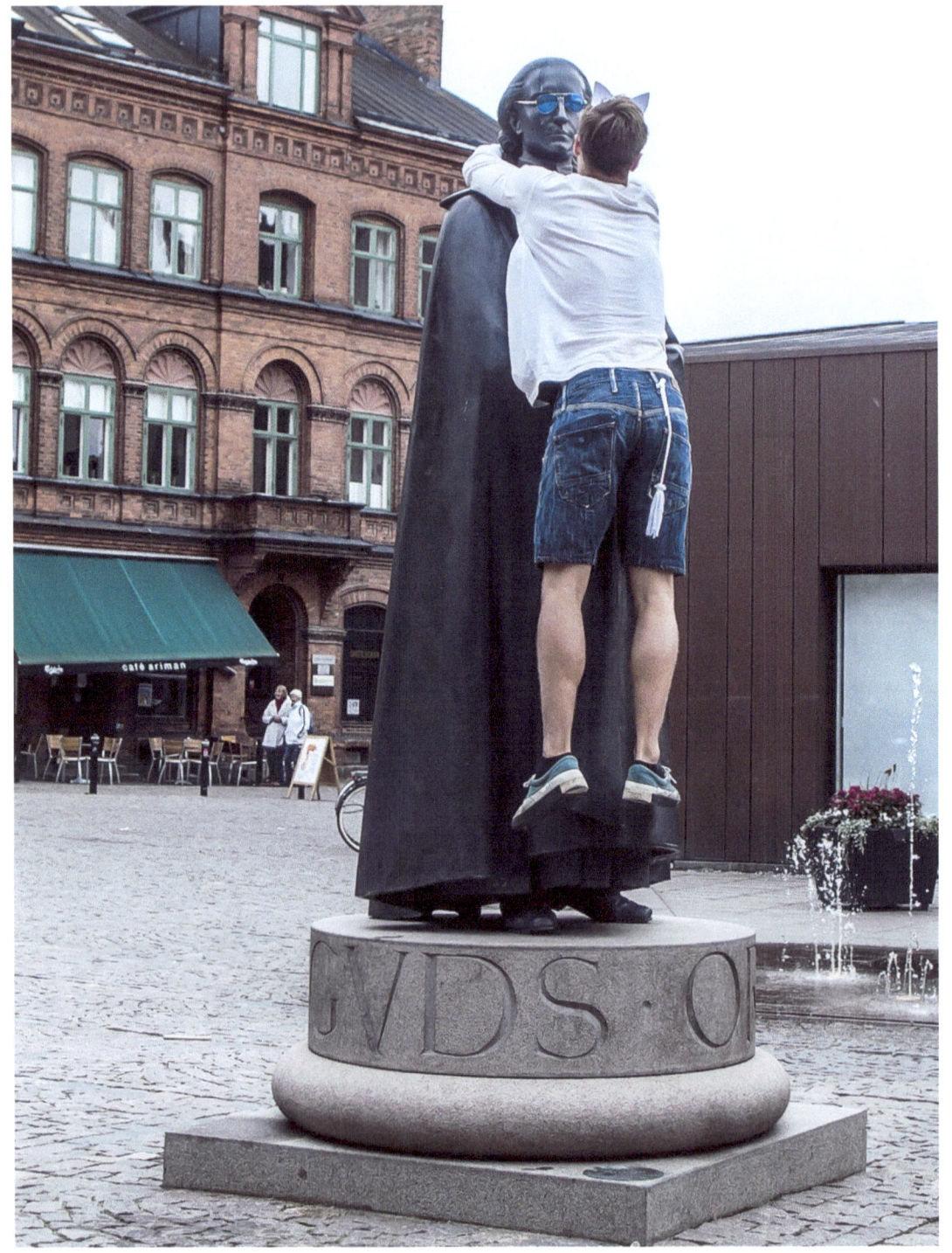

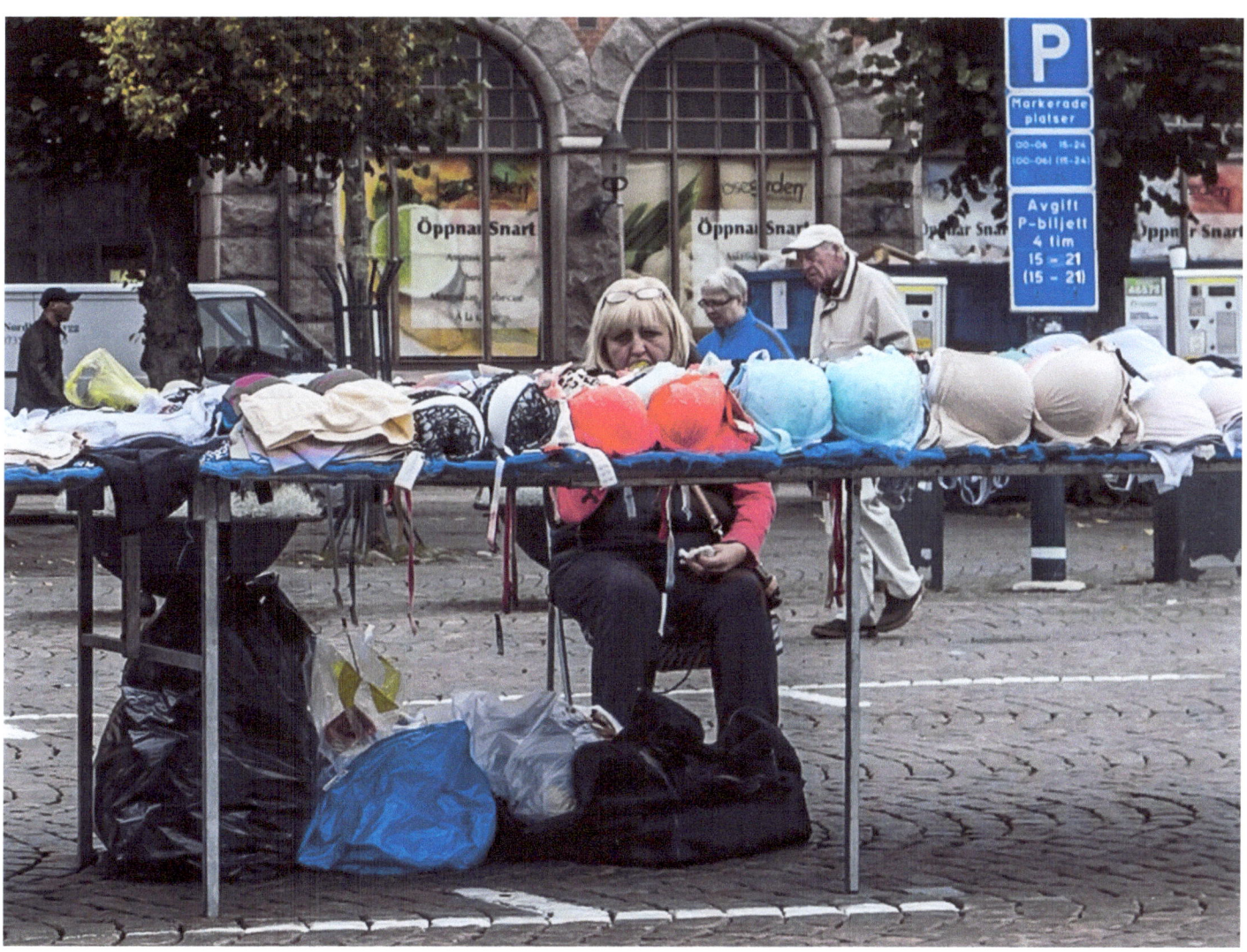

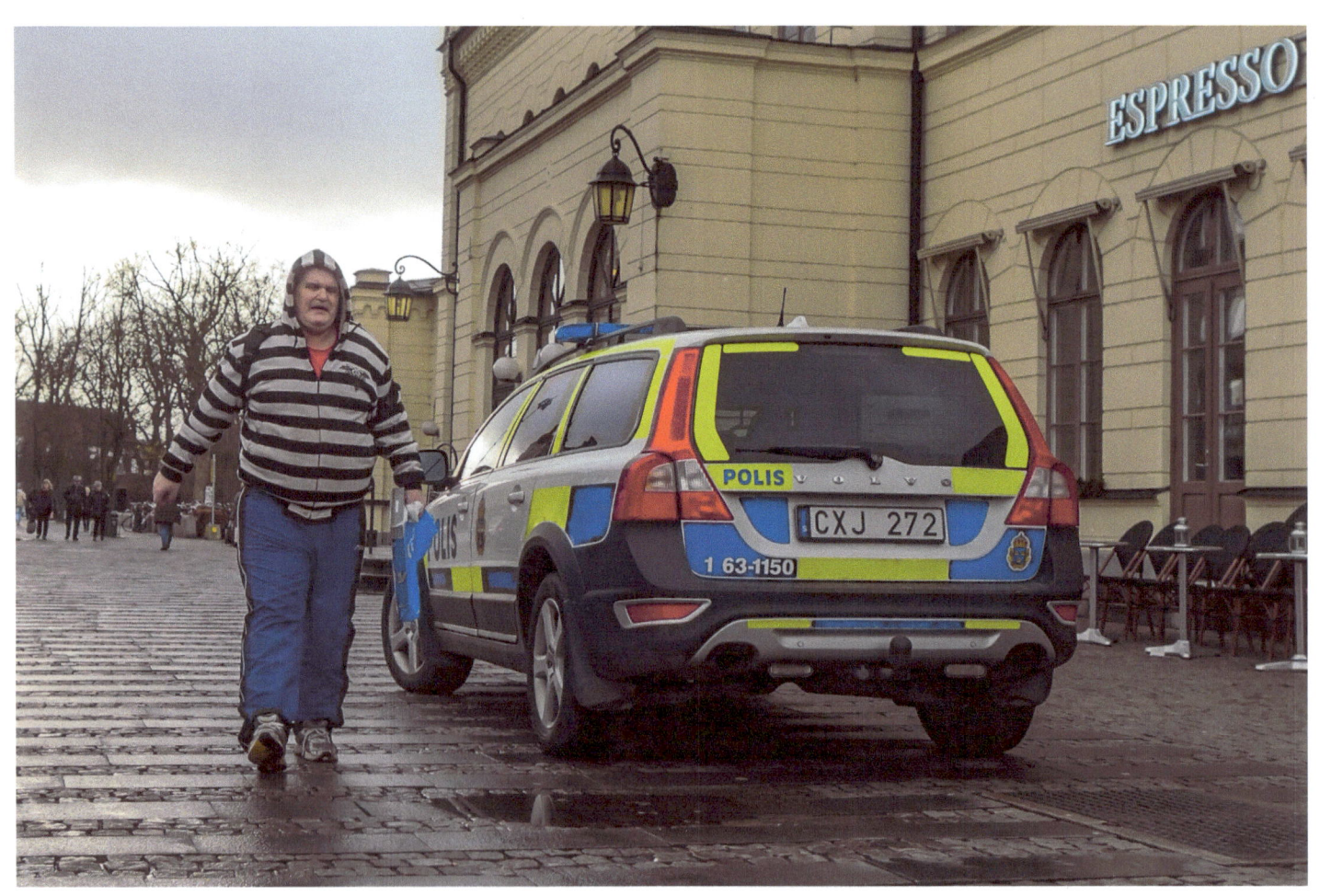

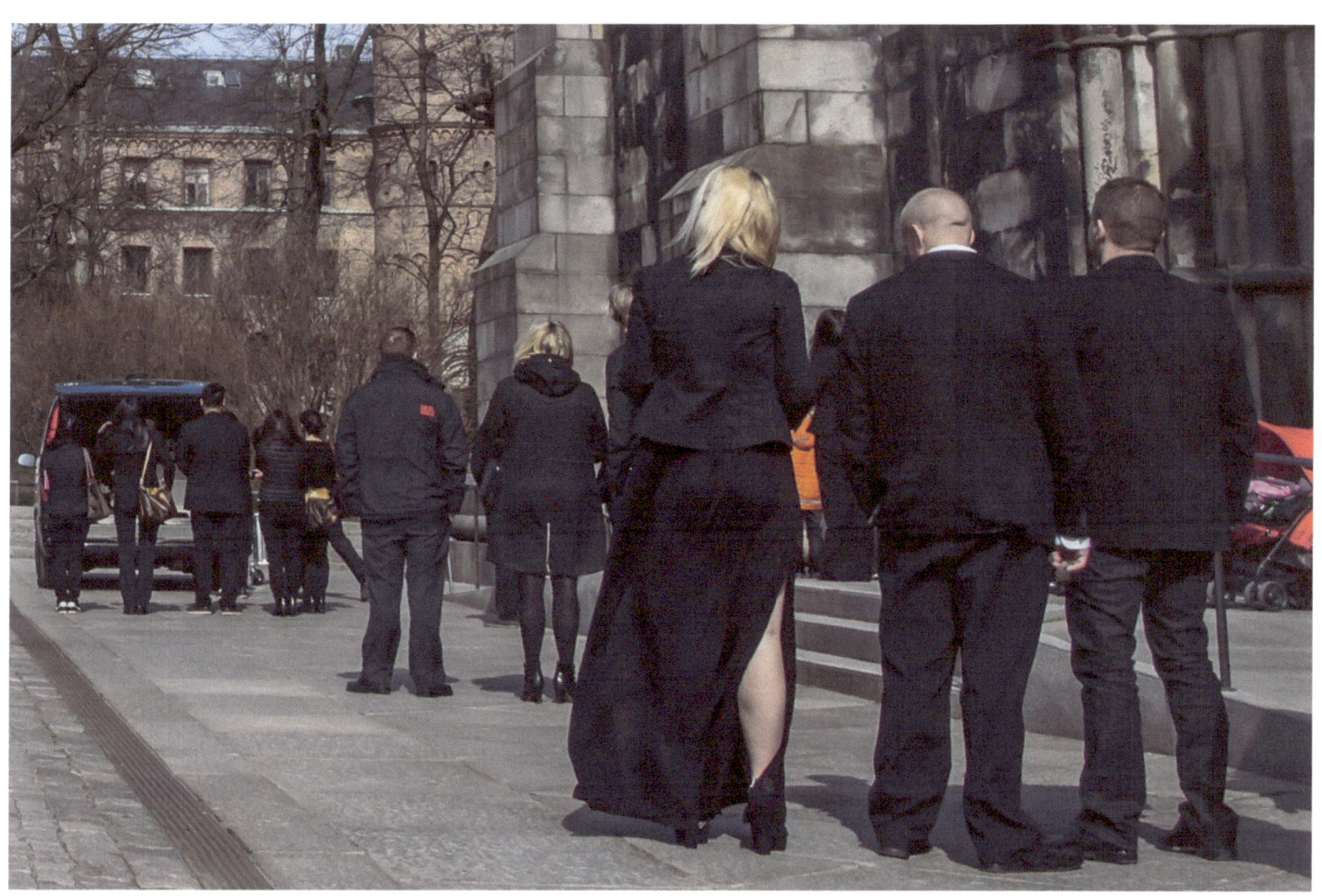

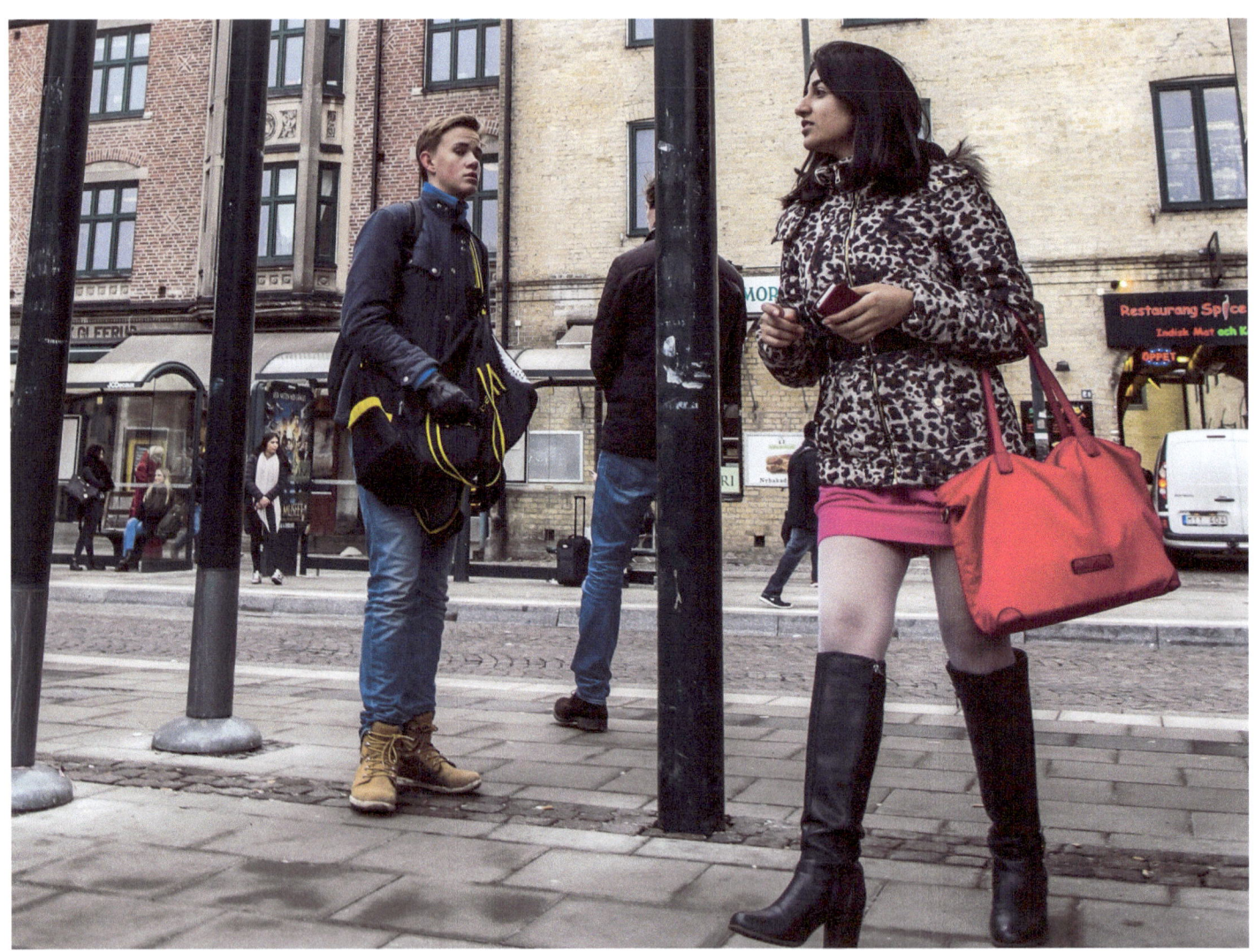

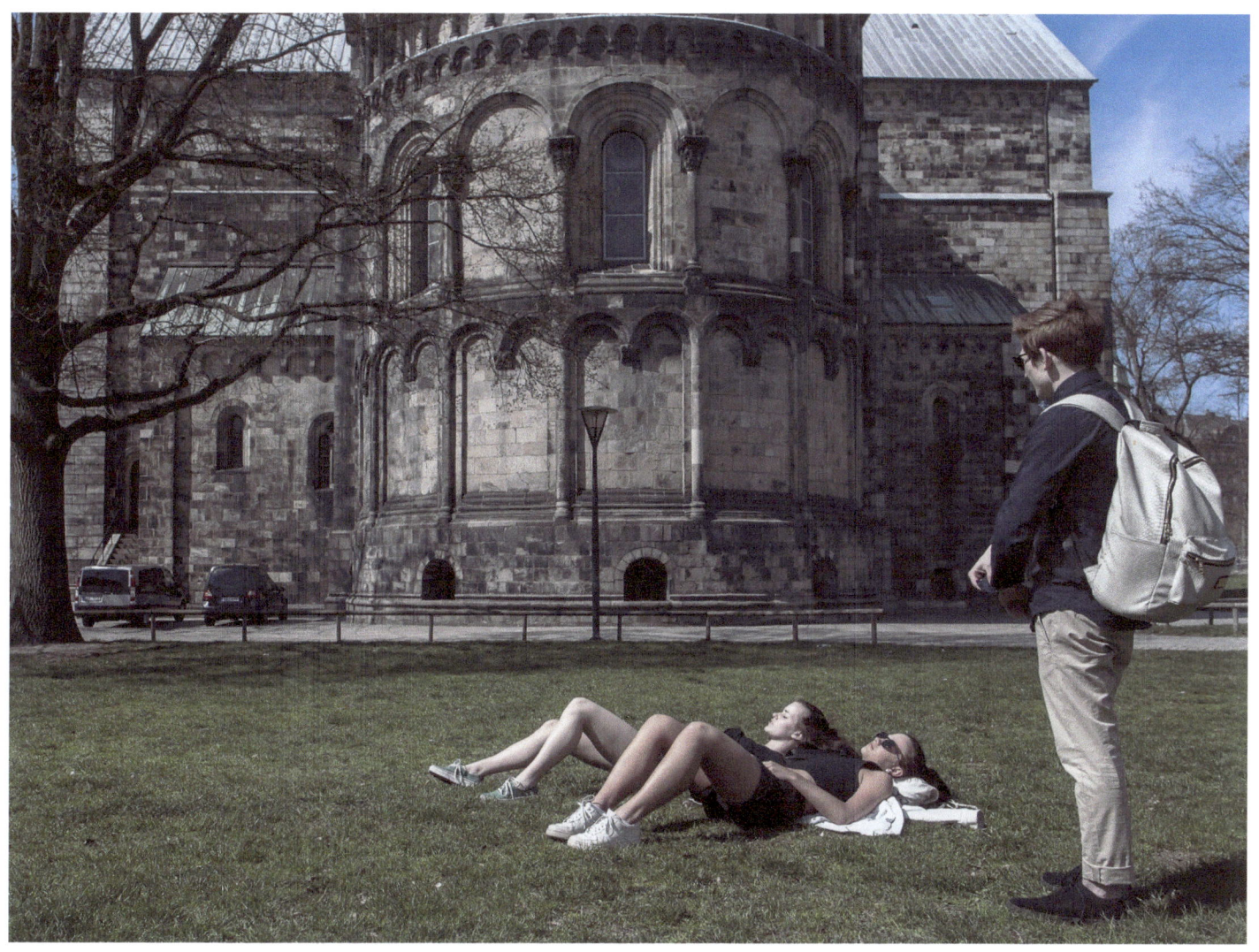

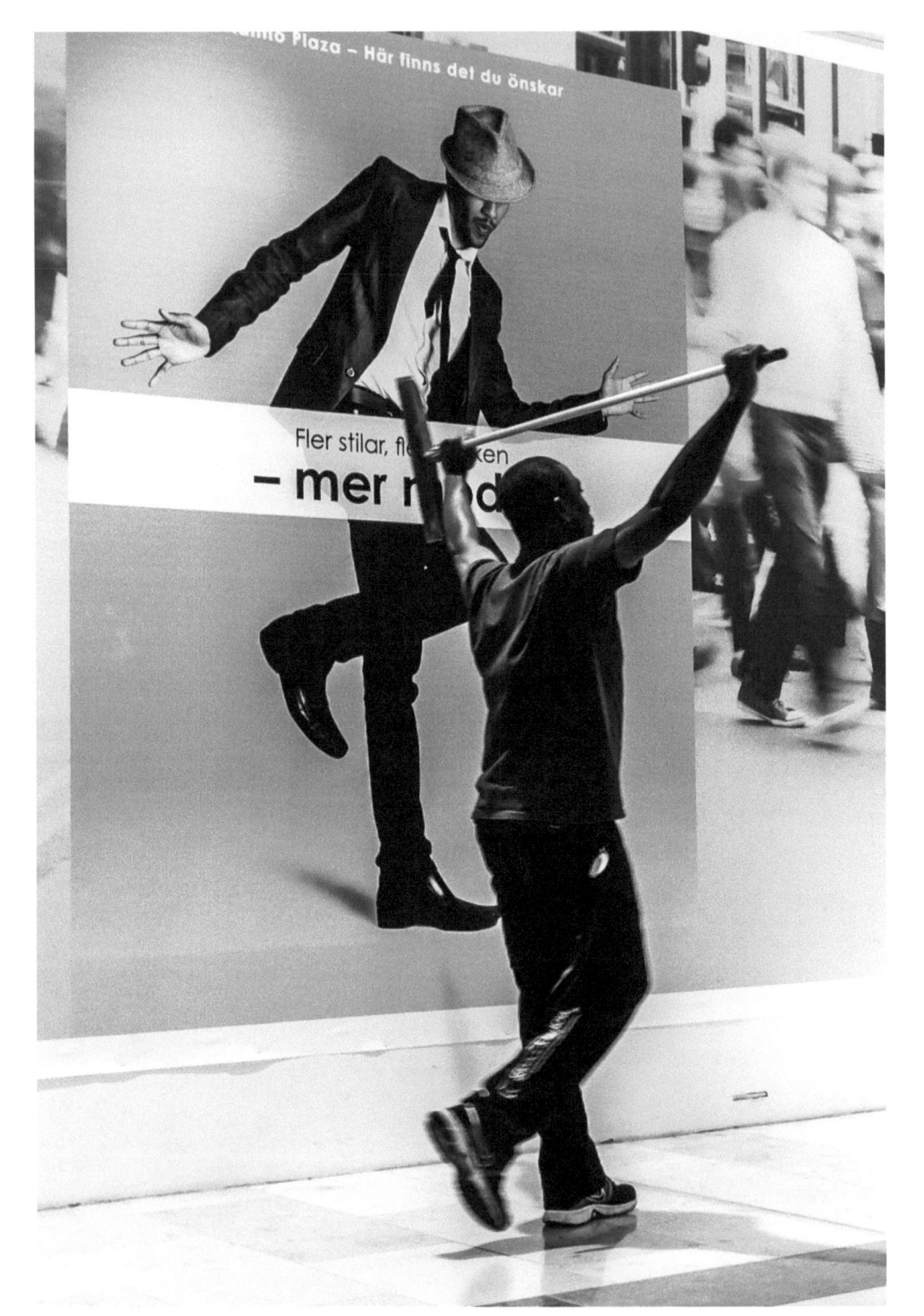

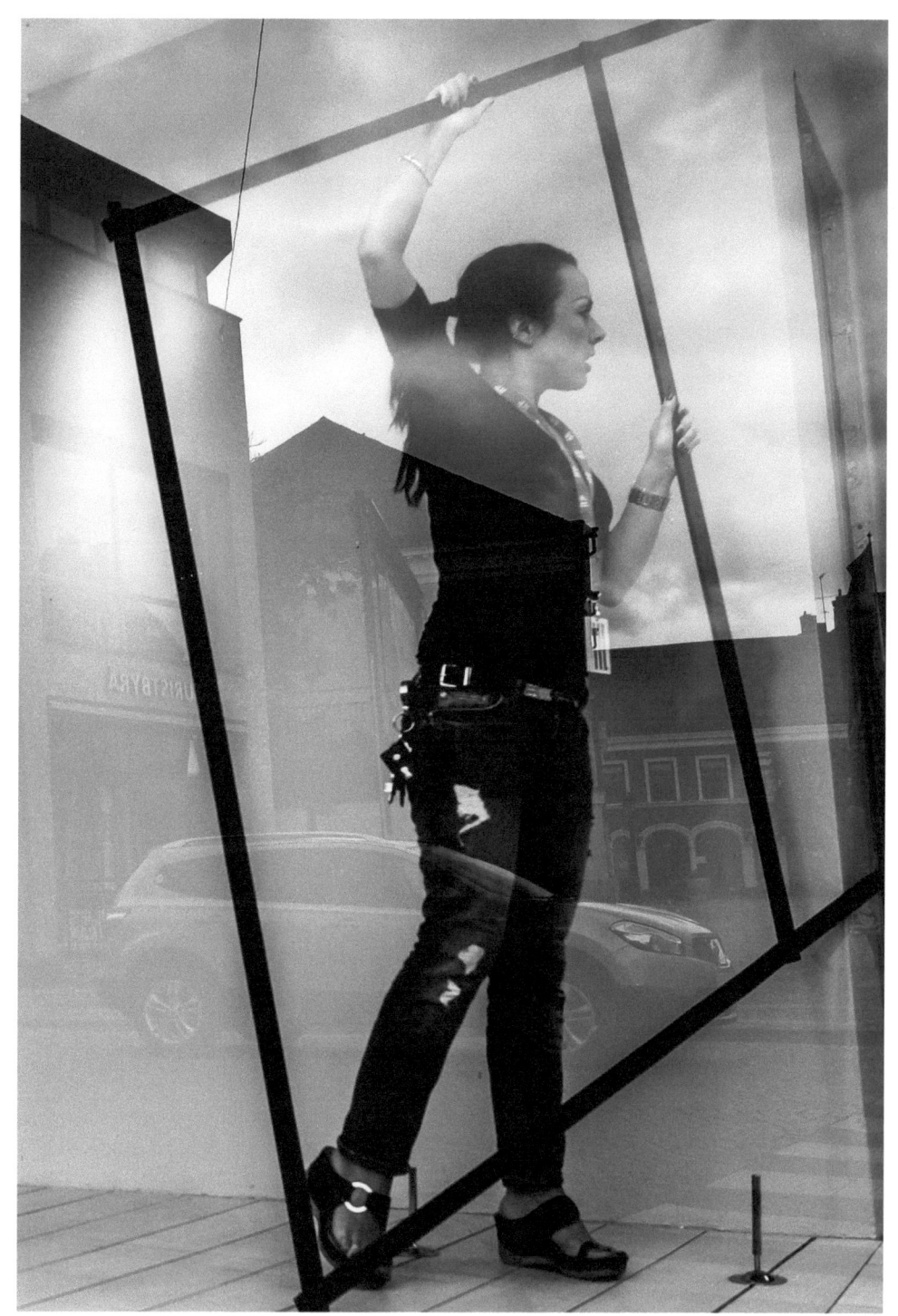

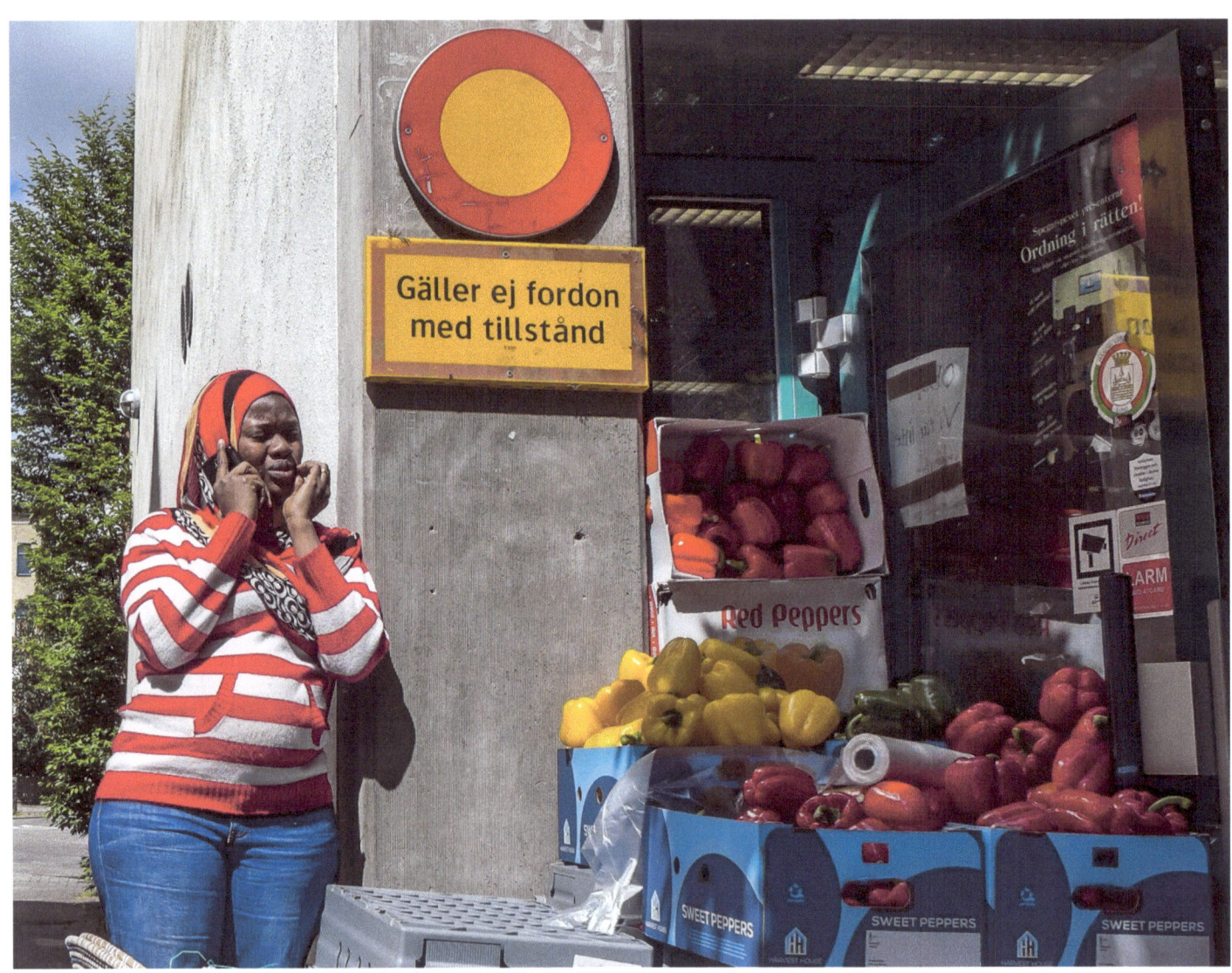

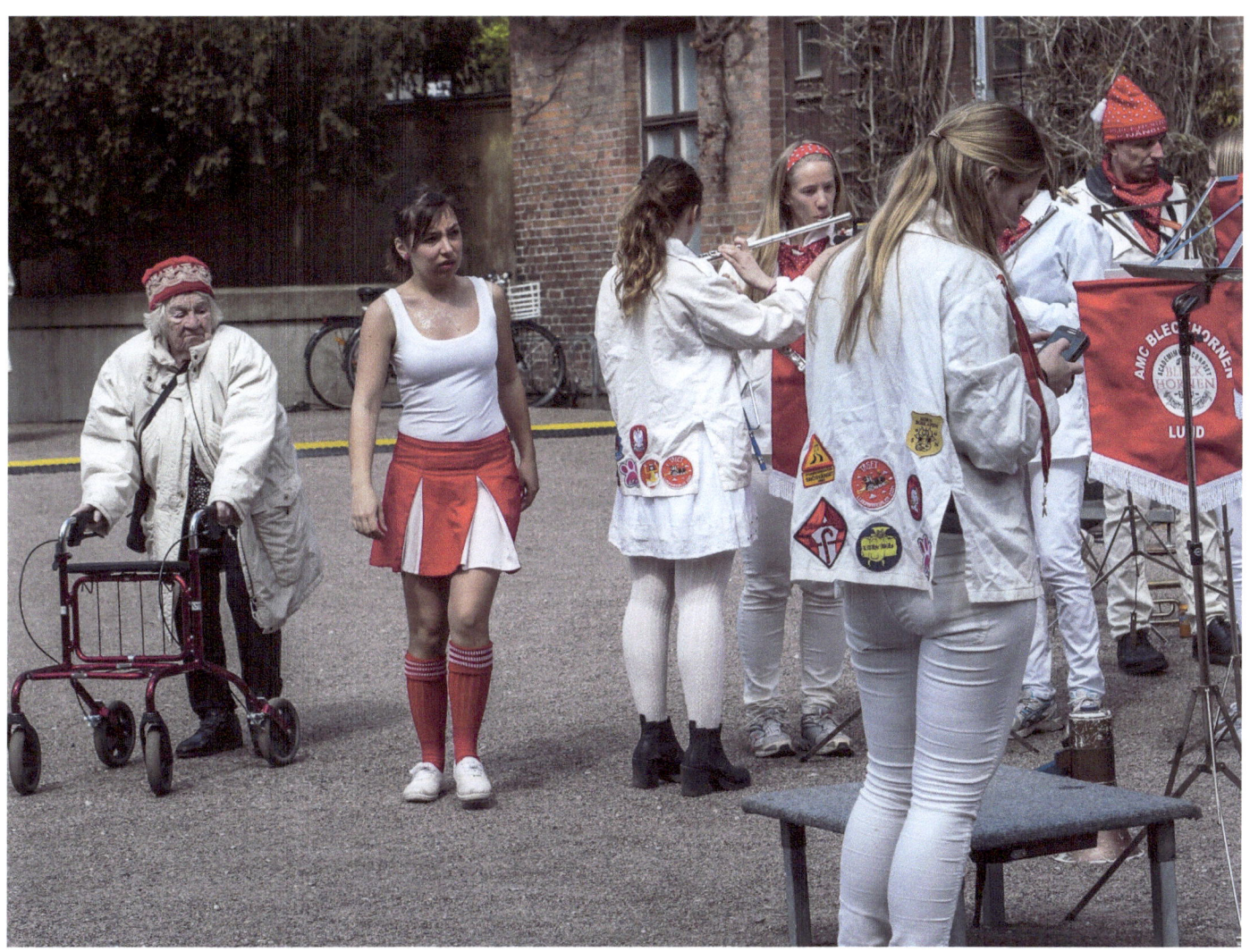

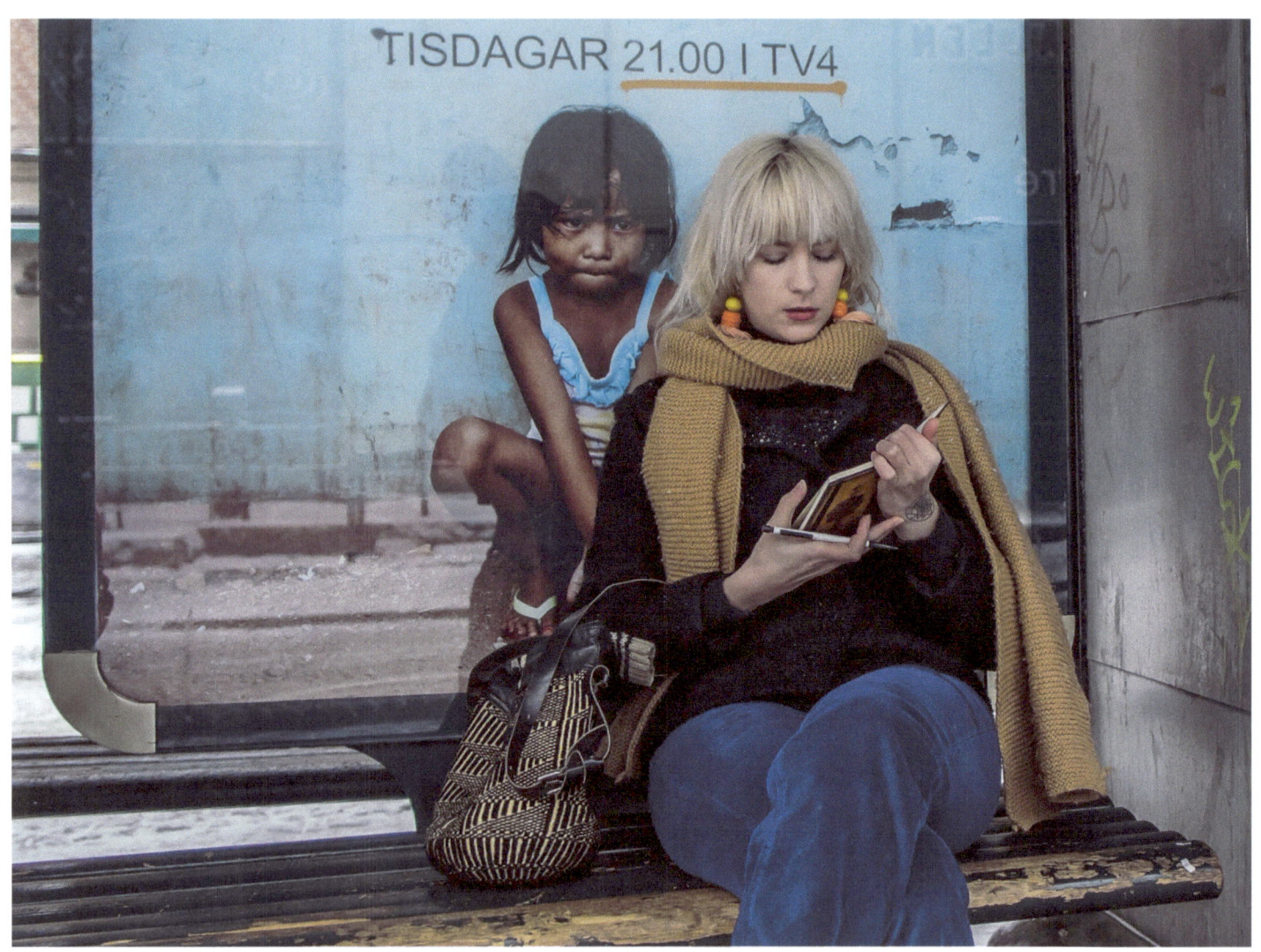

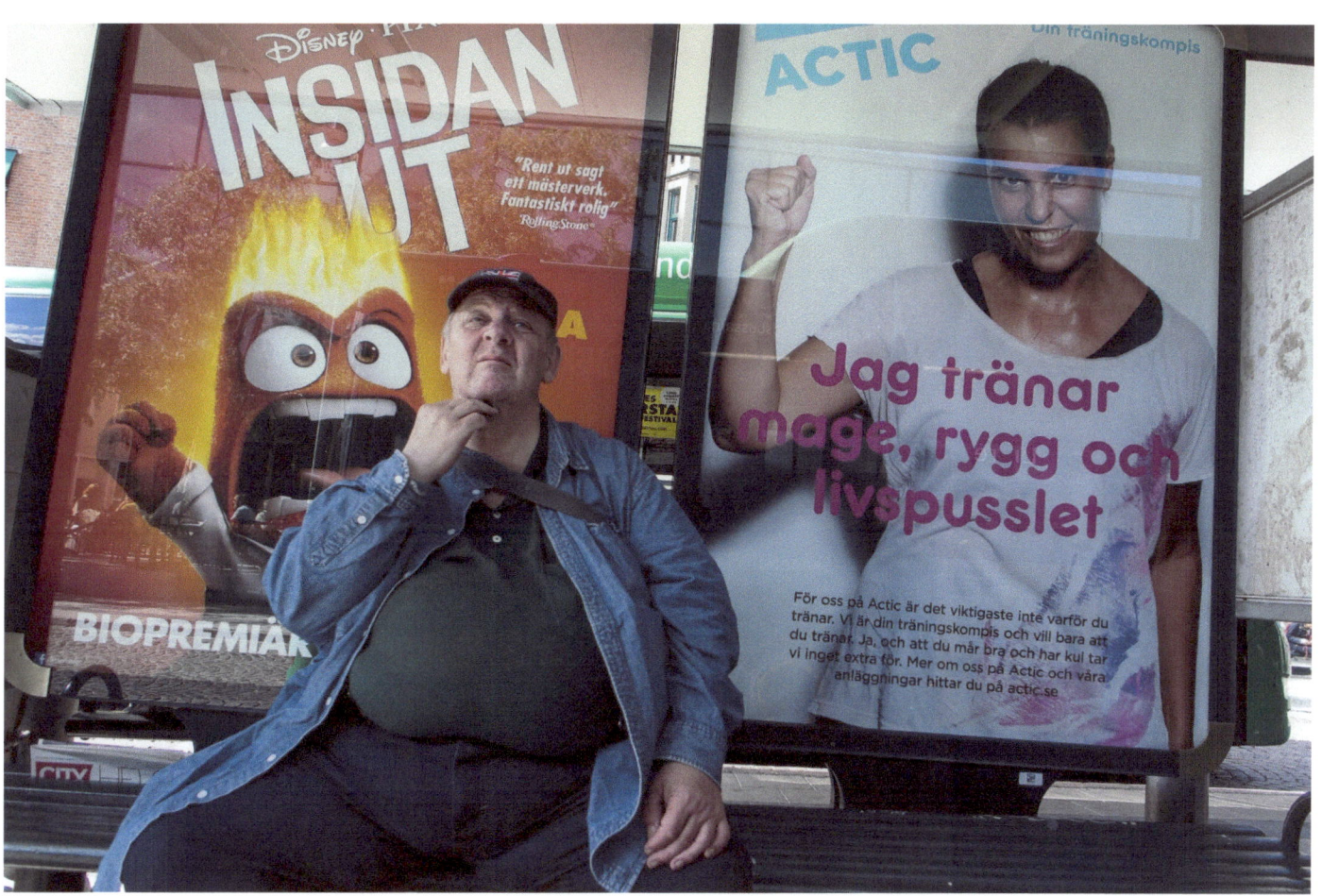

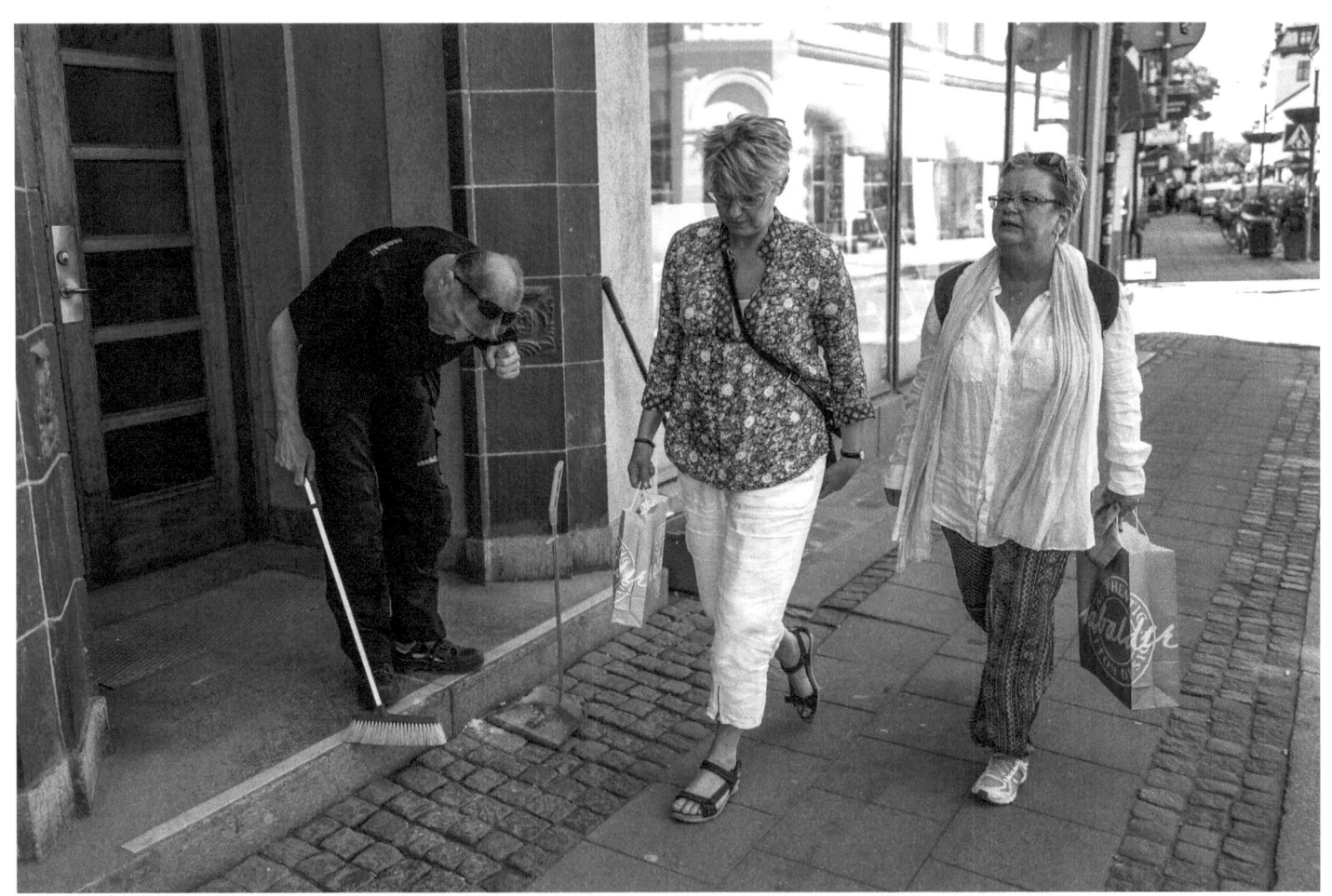

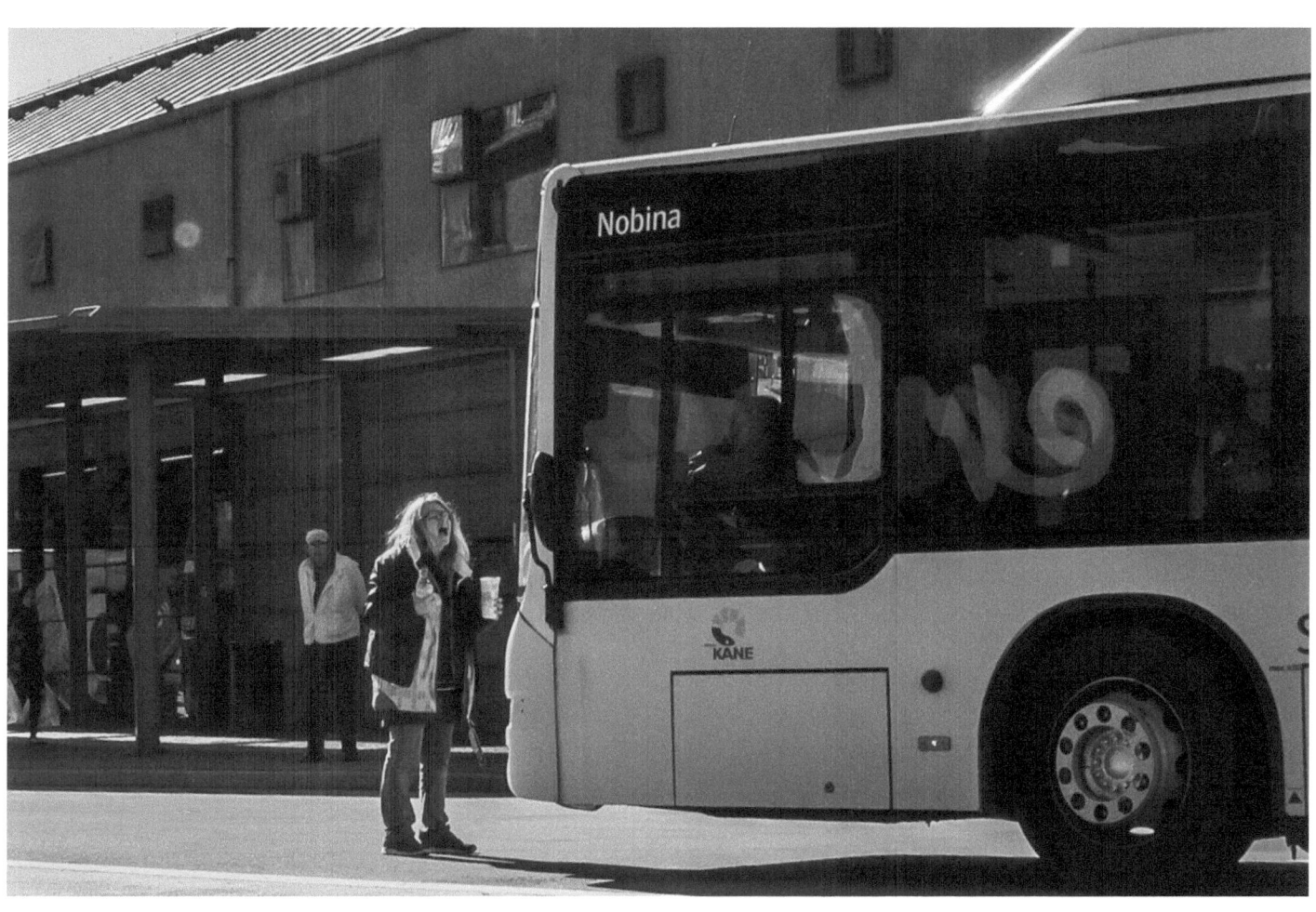

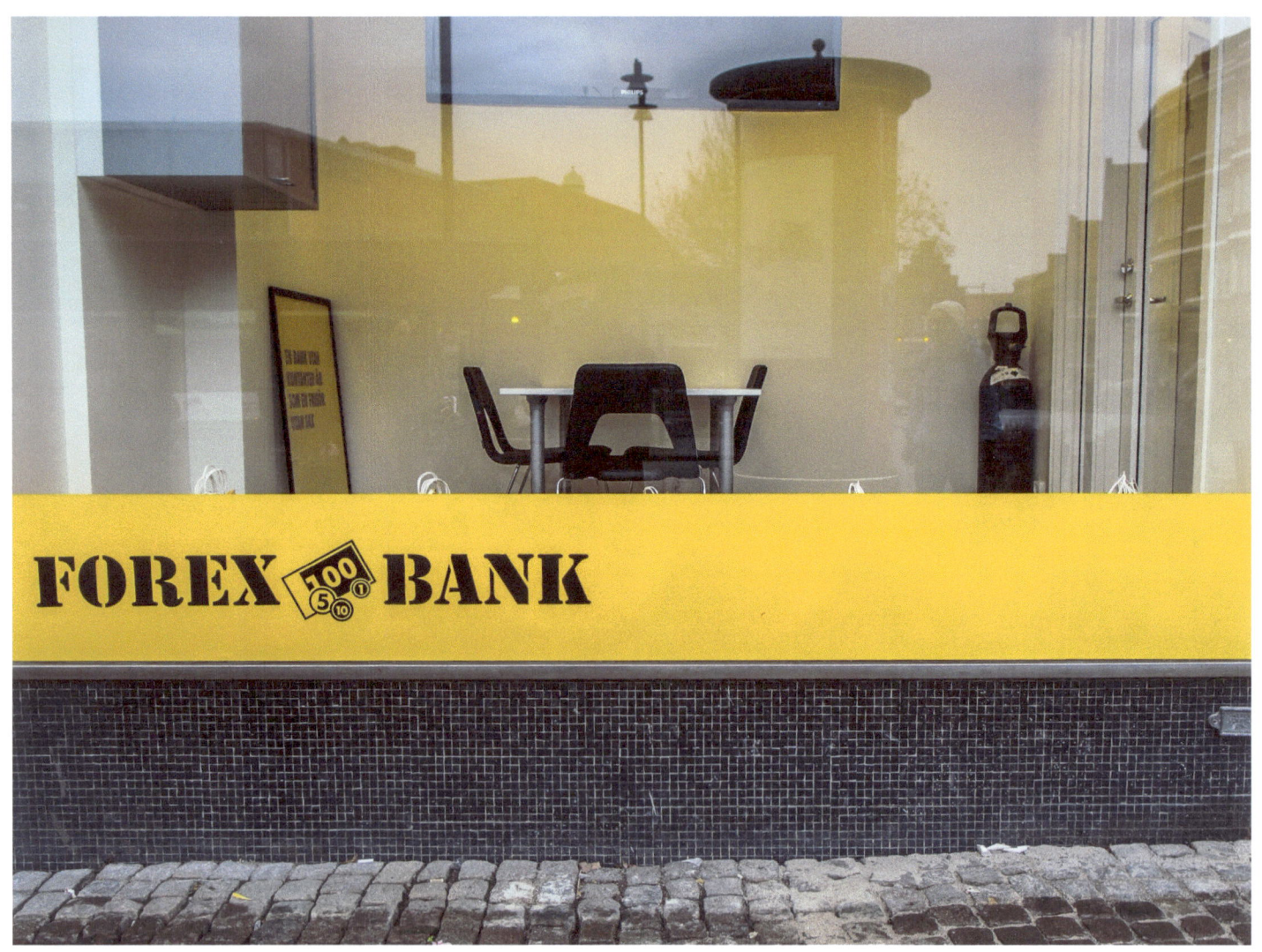

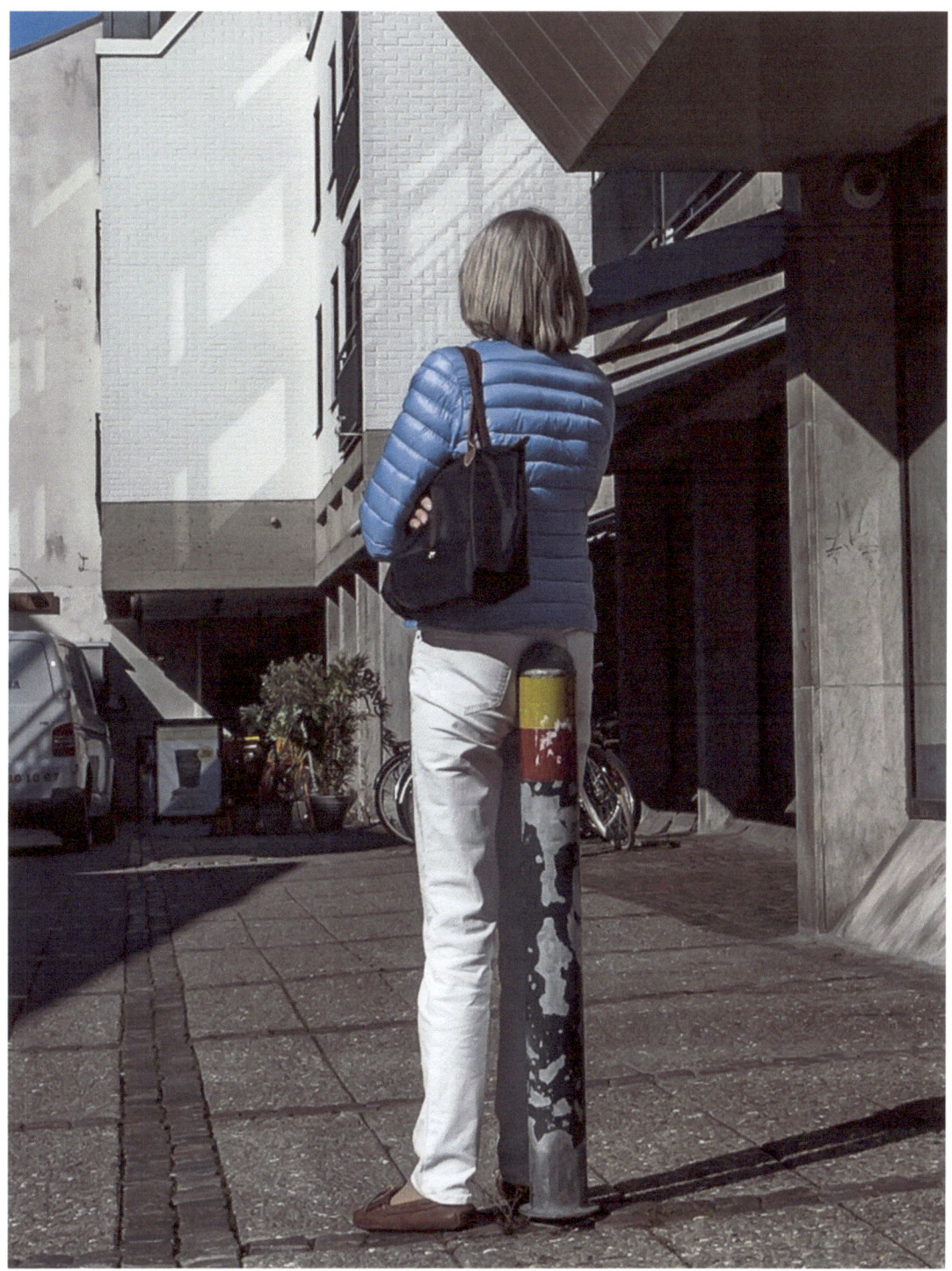

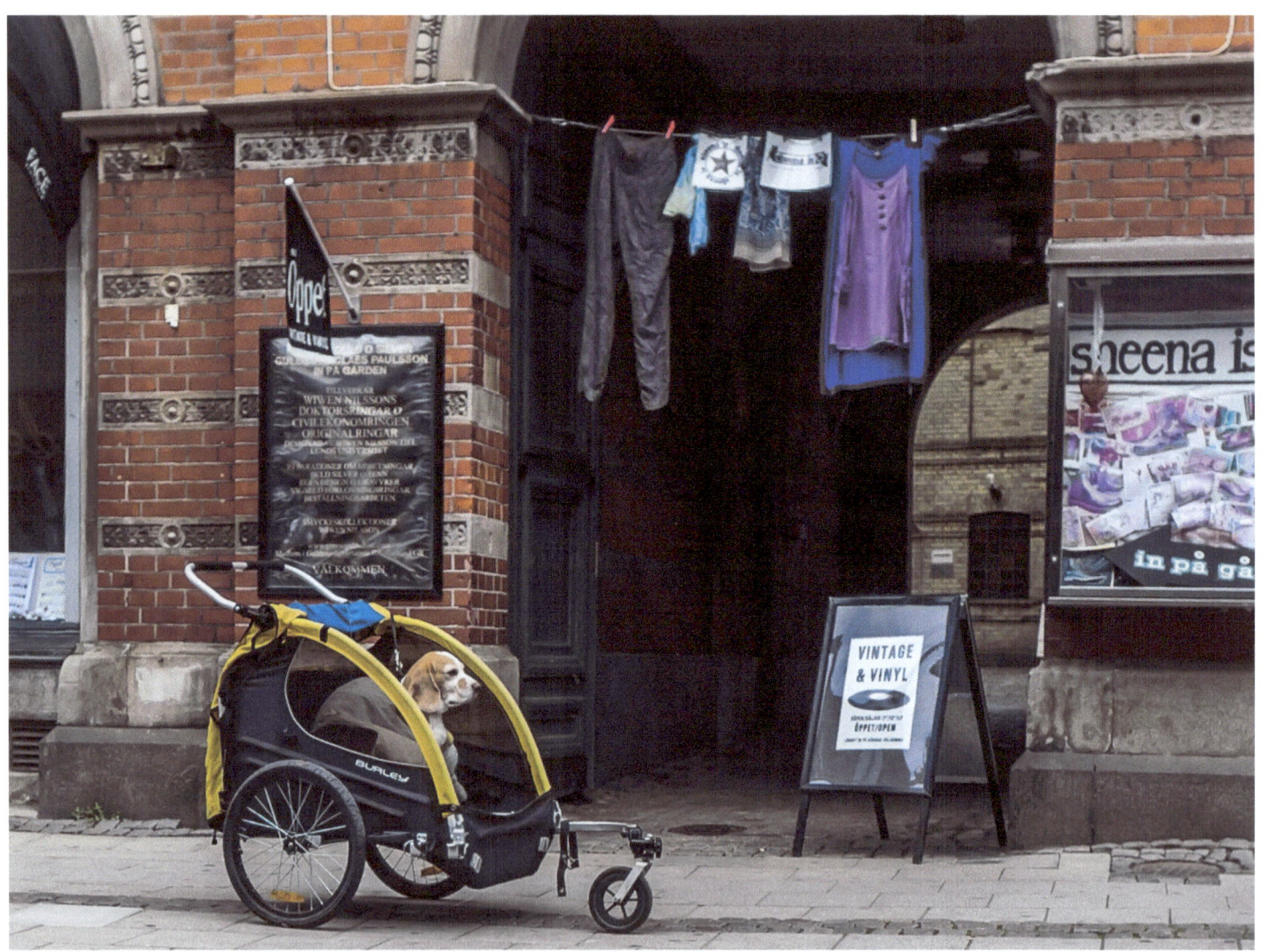

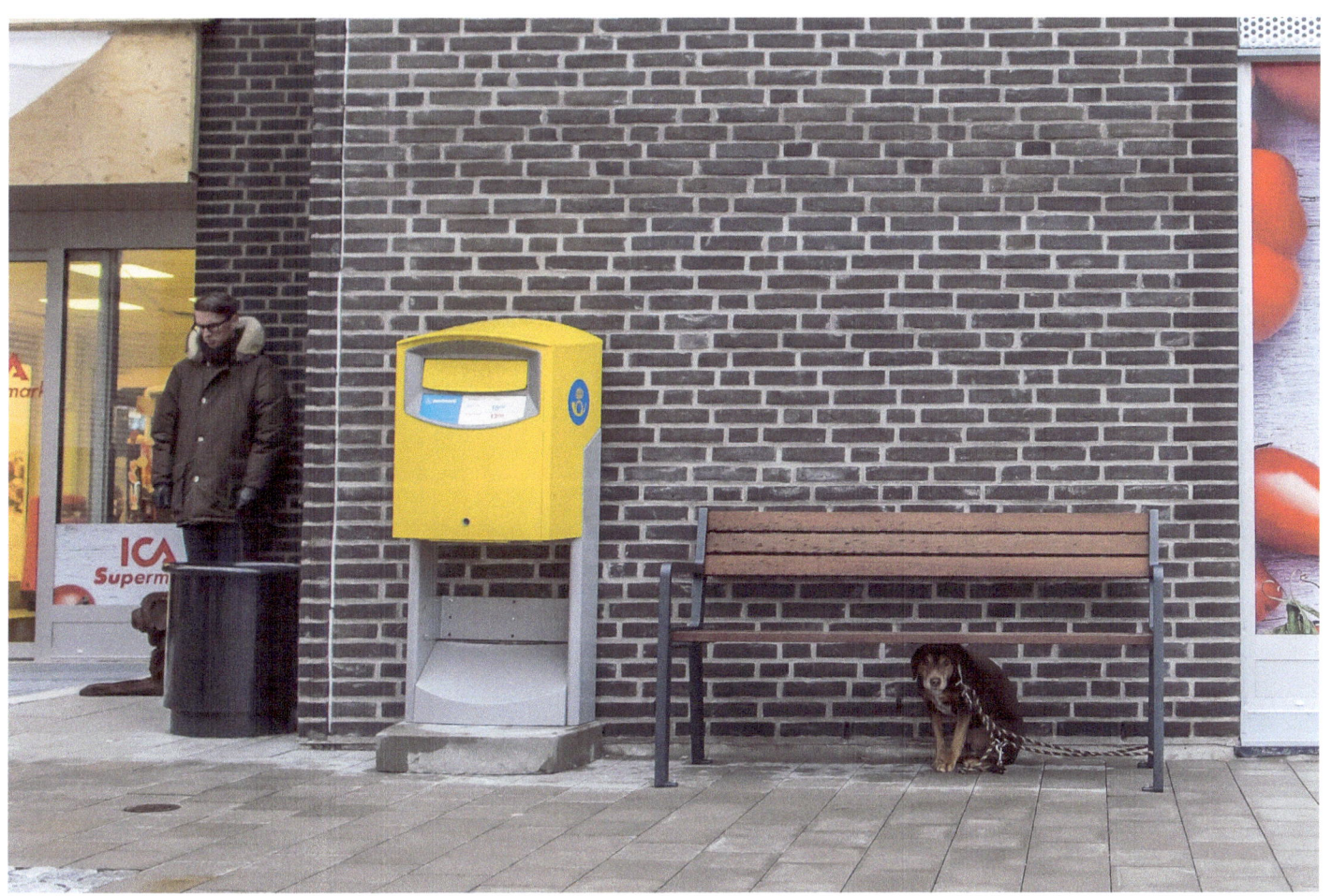

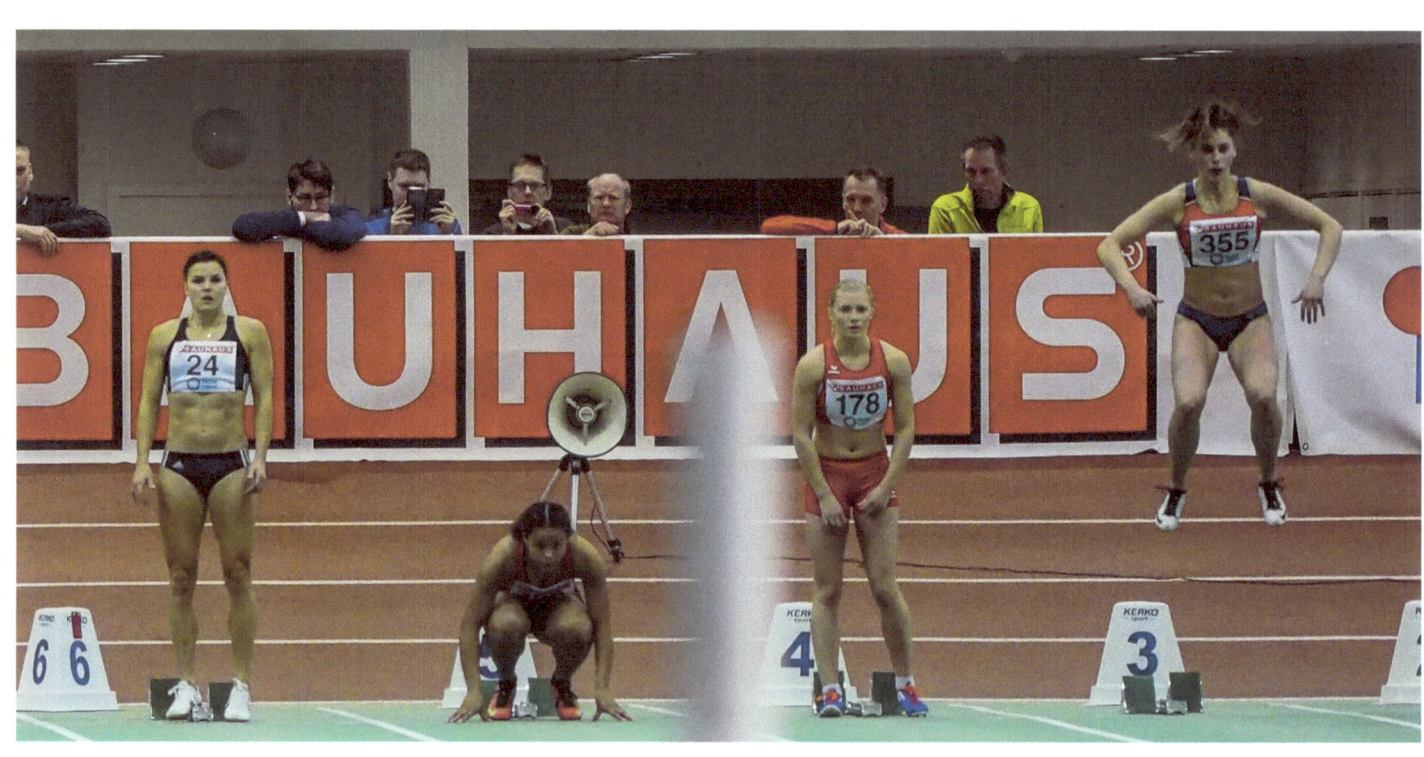

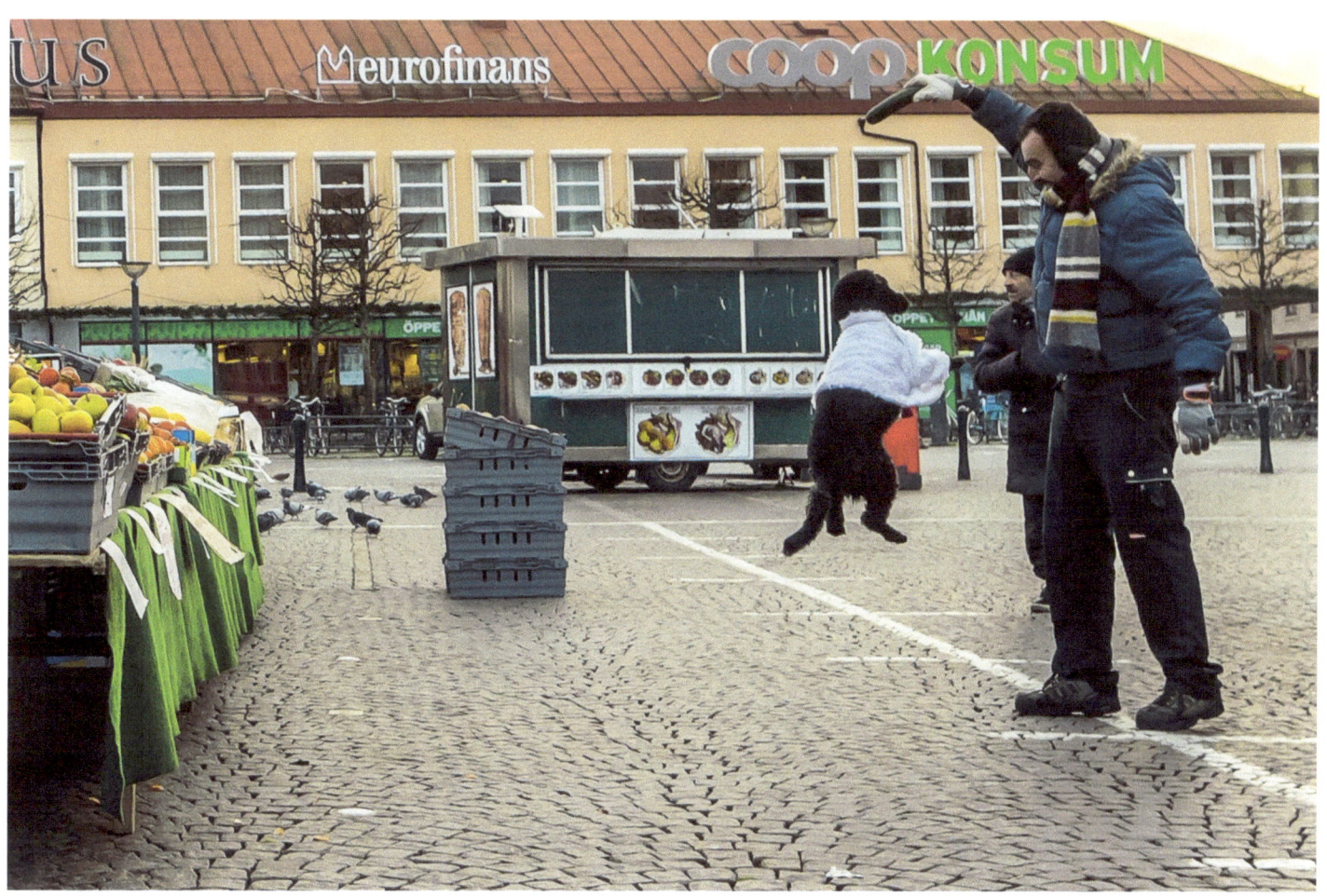

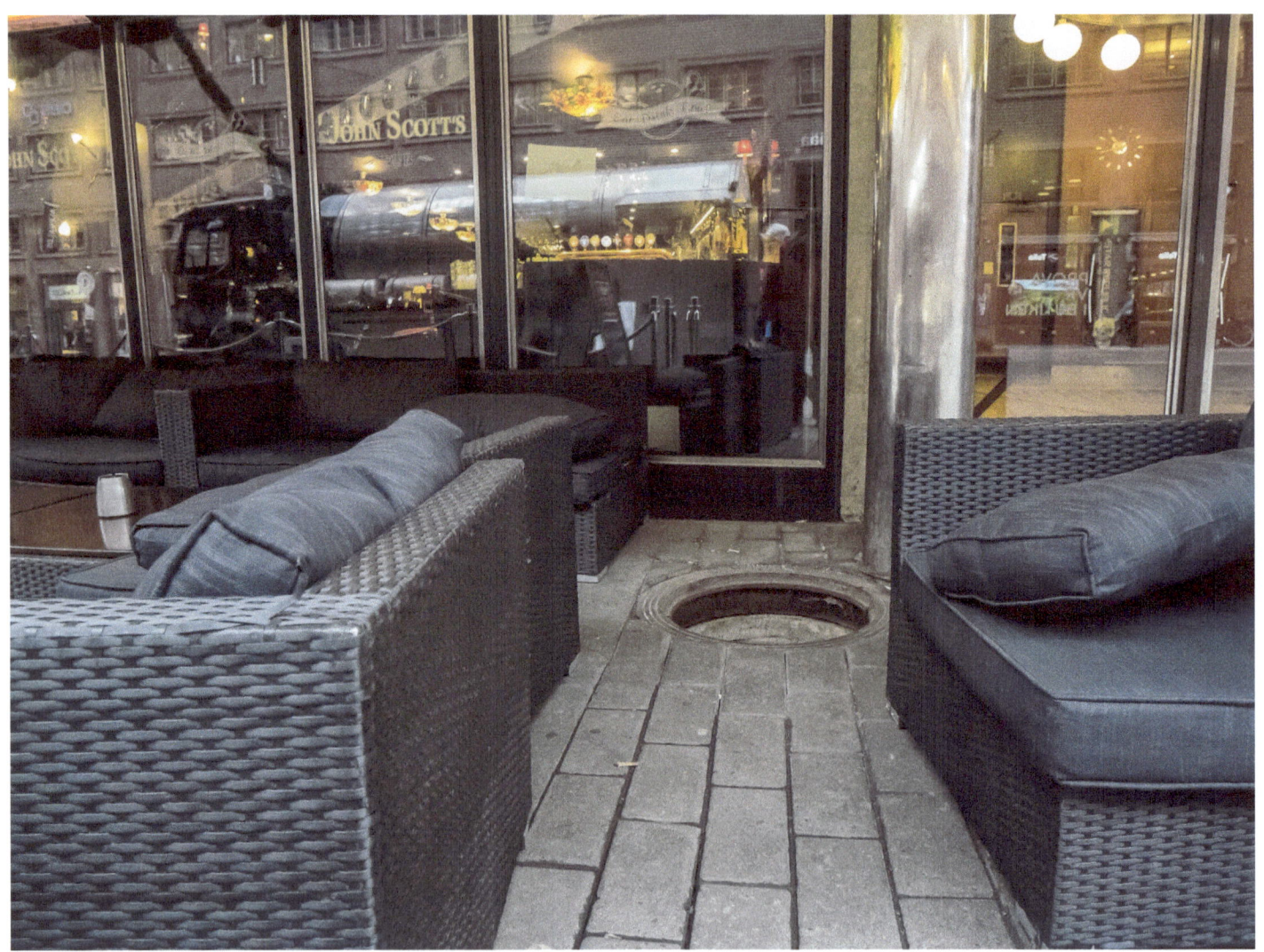

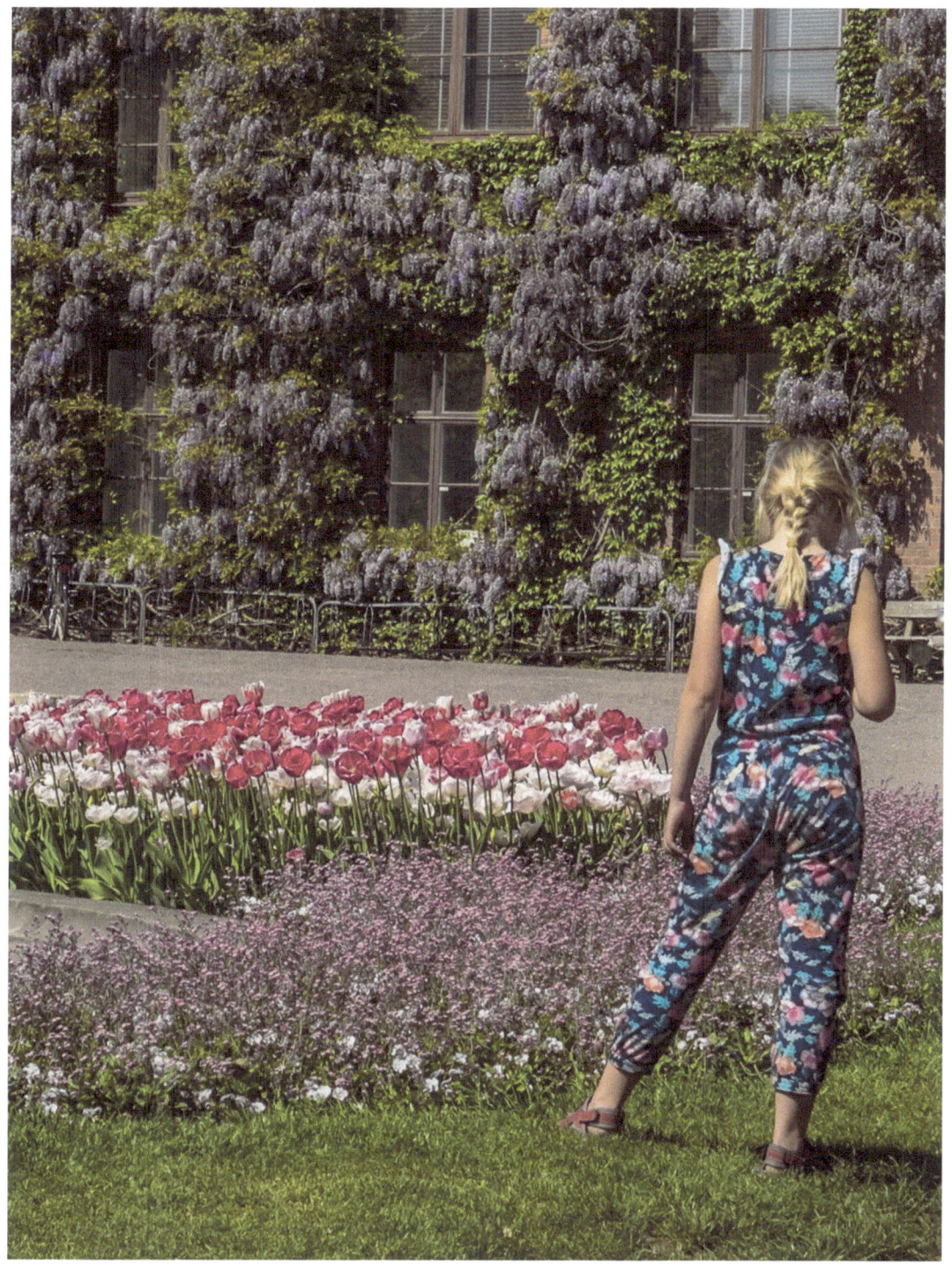

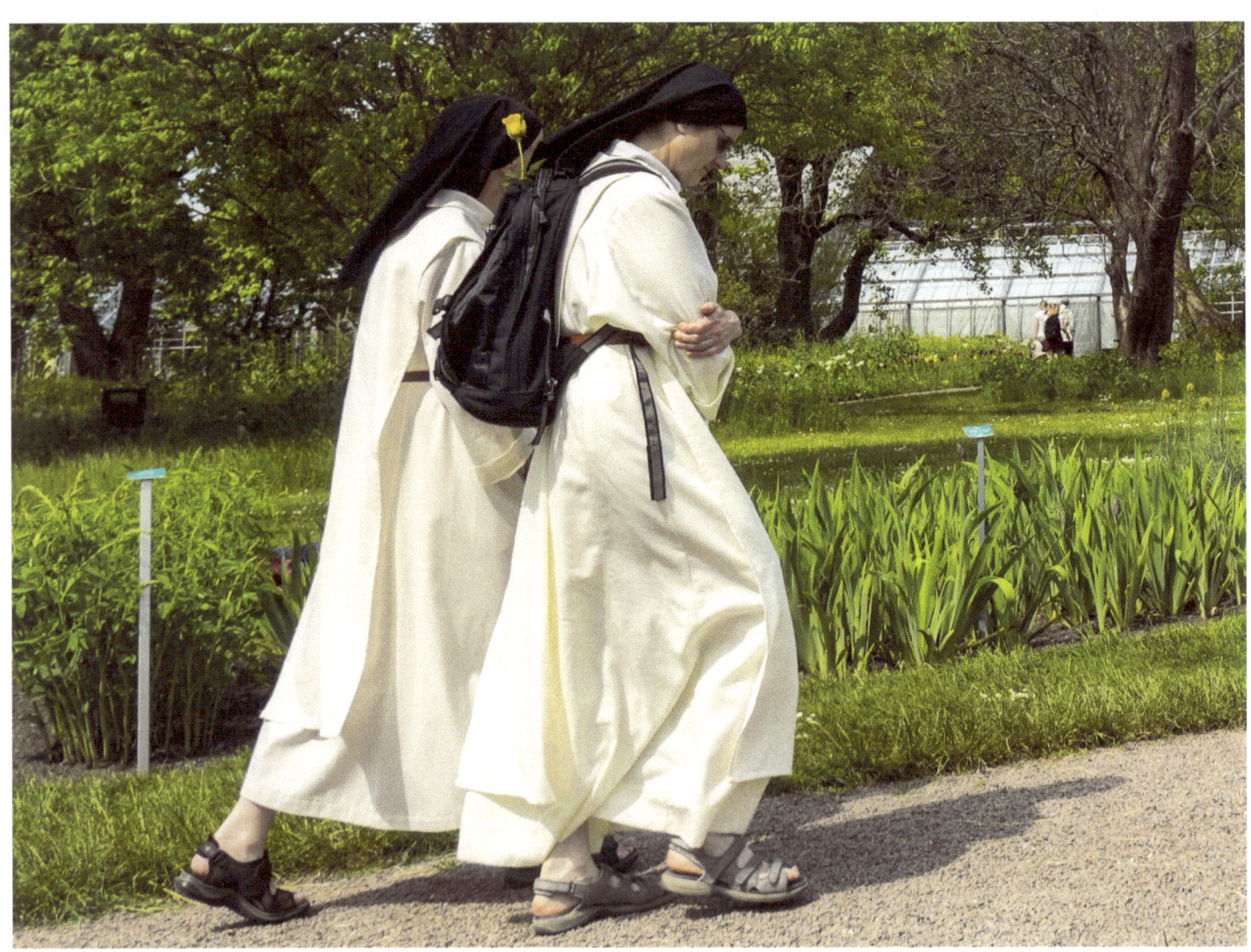

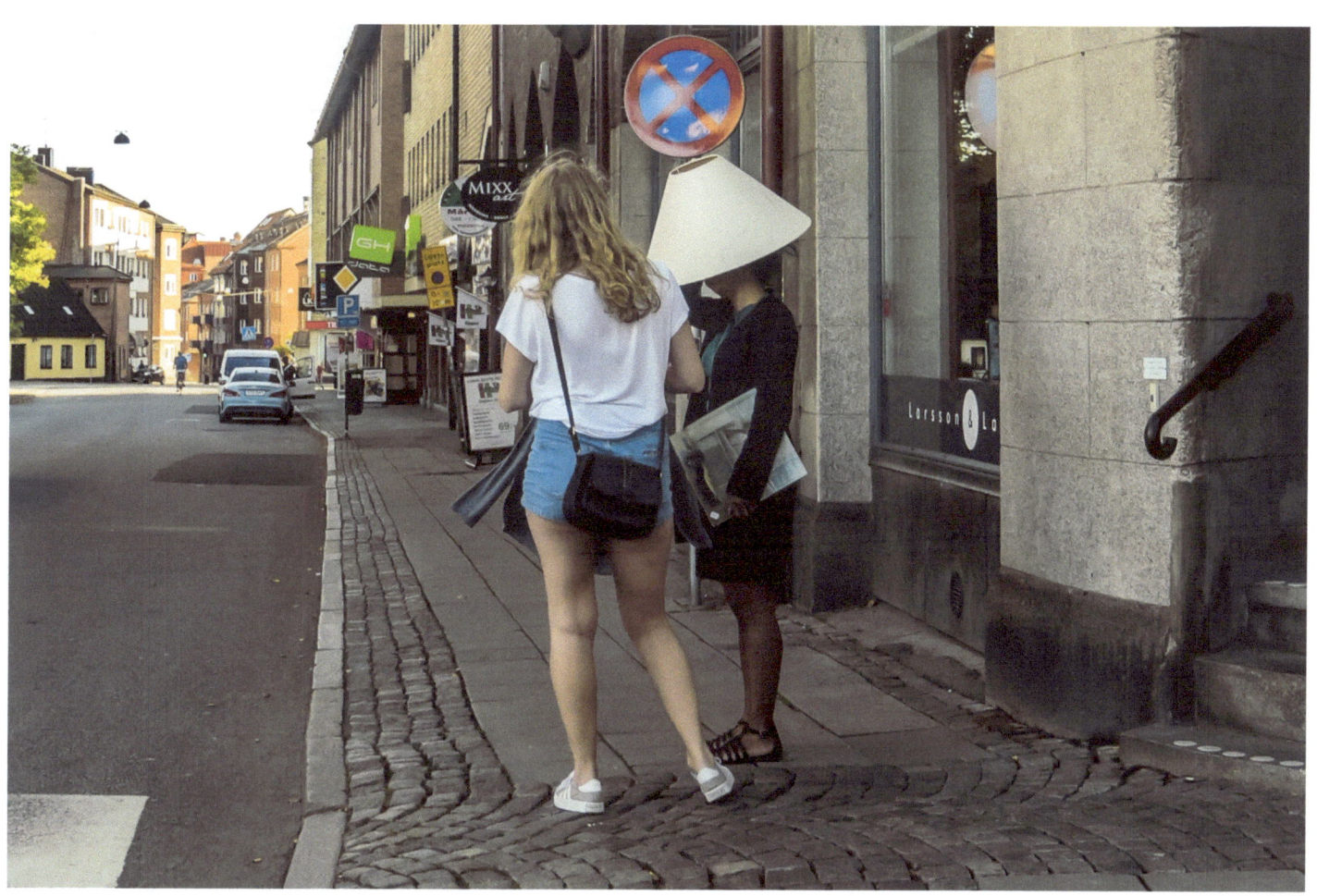

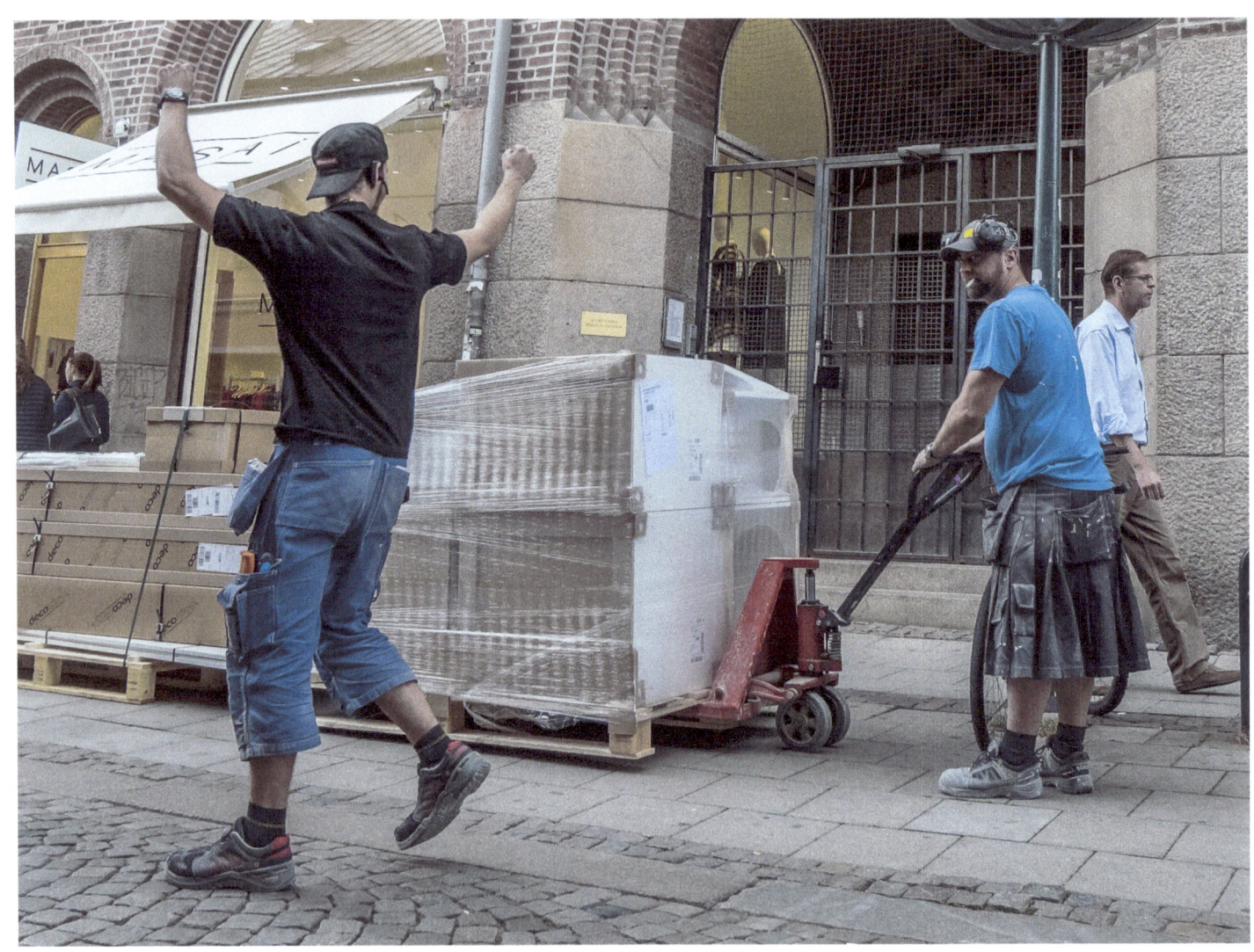

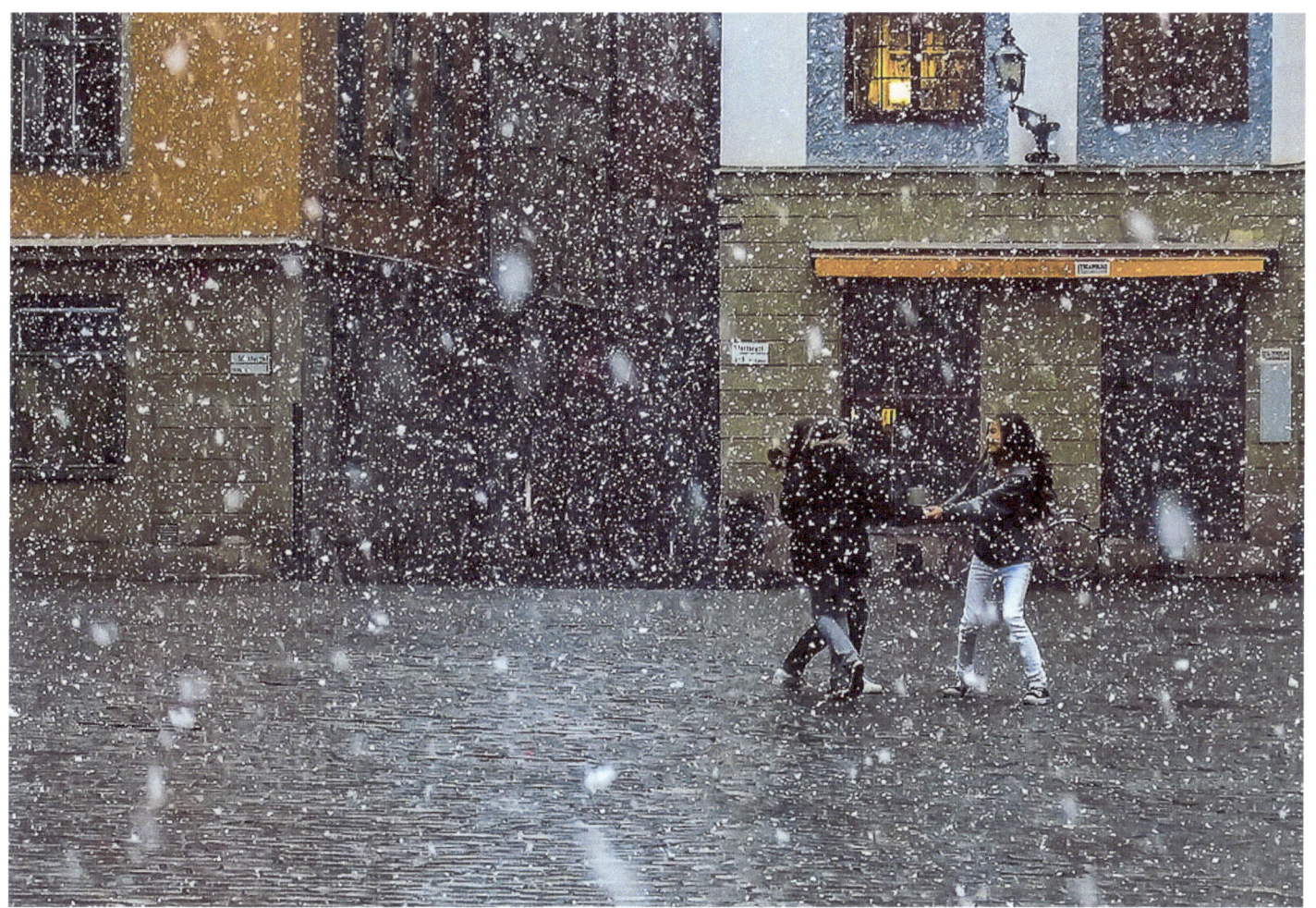

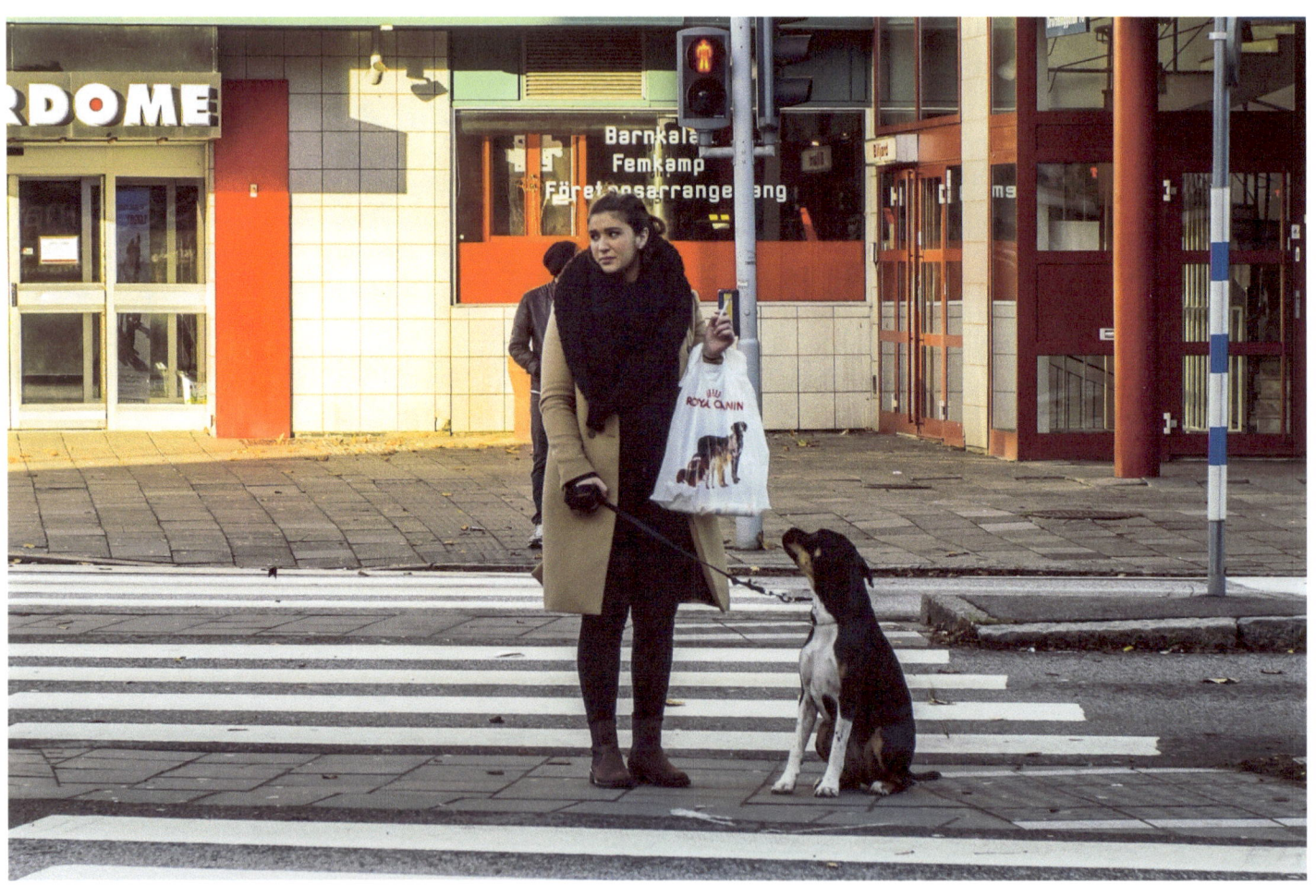

Bob Bovin in photography

Bob has been photographing since the middle of last century. He started with an Agfa Isolette and was already the 15-year-old freelance photographer at the local newspaper Corren and Östgöten. He got a picture rewarded best football image of the magazine Match 1958. His work as a freelance photographer aroused interest in documentary photography, which has followed Bob through life.
He have photographed people, environments and nature on all seven continents. Today, Bob is professor emeritus at the University of Lund and is a photographer full time. Nowadays he publishes books, both on paper and e-books. Bob has had solo photo exhibitions at the Östergötland County Museum and Scandinavian Photo in Bankeryd and Malmö. The most current project is to photograph polar bear and emperor penguins life on the edge of the ice, in order to highlight their role as indicators of environmental change.

Bovin Design Hb has published the following books:
New York remains. ISBN 978-1-4092-0178-6
En skola 1959. ISBN 978-91-978005-0-1
En skola 1959. e-book. ISBN 978-91-978005-1-8
Vårt skräp - framtidens fossil. e-book. ISBN 978-91-978005-2-5
Signs in situations. ISBN 978-91-978005-3-2
Humor i bilder. ISBN 978-91-978005-4-9
Humor i bilder. e-book. ISBN 978-91-978005-5-6
The Berlin Wall Falls. ISBN 978-91-978005-6-3
Berlinmurens fall. e-book. ISBN 978-91-978005-7-0
London 1967. A Photo Esaay. e-book. ISBN 978-91-978005-8-7